GRID A

C000131214

MAKING
CLOTH DOLLS

$\mathcal{M}$AKING
CLOTH DOLLS

EDITED BY
DOROTHEA HALL

CASSELL

First published in the UK
1994 by Cassell
Villiers House
41/47 Strand
London
WC2N 5JE

Copyright © 1994 Quarto Publishing plc
All rights reserved. No part of this book may be
reproduced or transmitted in any form or by any means,
electronic or mechanical, including photocopying,
recording or any information storage and retrieval
system, without prior permission in writing from the
copyright holder and publisher.

British Library Cataloguing-in-Publication Data
A catalogue record for this book is available from the
British Library.
ISBN 0 304 34363 3

This book was designed and produced by
Quarto Publishing plc
The Old Brewery
6 Blundell Street
London N7 9BH

Senior editor Kate Kirby
Senior art editor Amanda Bakhtiar
Designer Debbie Mole
Illustrators Elsa Godfrey, Sally Launder, Rob Shone
Photographer Chas Wilder
Dollmakers Rona Kemp 4-23 40-45 86-117,
Melanie Williams 24-39 46-85, Alicia Merrett 118-129
Consultant Janet Slingsby
Art director Moira Clinch
With special thanks to Sally Butler and Angela Faulkner

Typeset by West End Studios, Eastbourne
Manufactured in Hong Kong by Regent Publishing
Services Ltd
Printed in Hong Kong by Lee-Fung Asco Printers Ltd

SAFETY

1 When you buy fabrics, fillings and fittings, do make sure that they are from a reputable manufacturer who should have had to satisfy legal requirements re flammability etc.

2 If you intend to make a toy doll for a small child or baby it is safer not to use buttons, beads or any other decoration which can be pulled off and swallowed.

3 Do not under any circumstances use toxic paints, inks or dyes. Natural seed beads, especially the imported variety, should be avoided.

4 Joints should never be supported or attached with wire as this may eventually become loosened and pierce the fabric.

5 All commercial eye fastenings should be thoroughly checked to make sure that they have the necessary safety plates in place.

CONTENTS

BEFORE YOU START

PREPARATION OF FABRICS

With some of the bigger dolls you may wish to launder their clothes from time to time. Therefore, it is recommended that all new fabrics are washed and pressed before cutting out the pattern pieces. Gently hand wash in lukewarm soapy water (use mild soap flakes) and press between a clean towel before ironing dry. This will test for shrinkage and colourfastness.

AGEING NEW FABRICS

Character dolls such as the Attic dolls (page 58) are designed to look old and well loved. In order to achieve this effect, new fabrics should be steeped in strong tea before cutting out. Fill a sufficiently large bowl with cold, strong tea and immerse all the fabrics required for the project. Leave for one or two minutes, remove and squeeze out the excess fluid. While still damp, press with a hot iron. This has the effect of scorching the fabric which also adds to the 'antique' look.

TRACING ACTUAL-SIZE PATTERN PIECES

When the pattern pieces are given actual size, you can simply photocopy them from the book and cut out the copy. If a photocopying service is not available, make your own copy using tracing paper. Place the tracing paper on top of your chosen pattern securing the edges firmly with paper clips or bulldog clips and, with a pencil, draw around the pattern outline. Use a ruler for all straight lines. Copy all marks and information and cut out your traced pattern piece using general purpose scissors. (For pattern pieces that need to be enlarged see the box opposite.)

CUTTING OUT PATTERN PIECES

When you have cut out all the paper pattern pieces for your chosen project and marked and labelled them, the next step is to follow the fabric cutting layout. First determine how the fabric has been folded, if at all. You will notice, in some instances, that the fabric has been folded leaving a layer of single fabric to one side.

1 Working on a flat surface, arrange your pattern pieces on the appropriate fabric as shown in the diagram. Pin them in place, pinning the straight grainline first. Cut out using sharp dressmaker's shears.

2 Clip into the seamline to show the centre front (CF) and centre back (CB) on the appropriate pattern pieces. Transfer balance marks, darts and, on some doll patterns, the face and shoe details, using dressmaker's carbon paper.

3 To trace the marks, place the waxed side of the carbon paper to the wrong side of the fabric – you may have to remove a few pins. Trace the markings on with a tracing wheel and ruler using short, firm strokes.

4 When transferring face and shoe details, work freehand with the carbon paper placed waxed side to the right side of the fabric, underneath your tracing. Use a soft pencil or empty ball point pen for tracing.

ENLARGING PAPER PATTERN PIECES

The half-size pattern pieces given for some of the projects in this book need to be enlarged before you can pin the pattern pieces onto the fabric. The easiest method is to use a photocopier.

Using a photocopier: set the machine to enlarge the copy by 200% then photocopy the required pattern pieces. Once enlarged, cut out the paper pattern pieces and pin them onto the fabric.

USING THE GRID METHOD

If a photocopier is not available, then the pattern pieces can be enlarged using the grids supplied with this book.

1 Trace off the small grid (A) which you will find at the beginning of this book.

2 Place the traced-off grid on top of the pattern pieces you wish to enlarge and trace them off.

3 On a separate sheet of paper, trace off the large grid (B) which you will find at the back of this book.

4 The pattern pieces traced off onto the grid. Note all construction points and information have been transcribed.

Using grid A as a point of reference, mark on grid B the points where the outline of the pattern crosses the grid lines then join up these marks to complete the pattern shapes. Add all construction points and information, then cut out the paper pattern pieces and pin them to the fabric.

MACHINE STITCHING

Before making the dolls, it is advisable to check the stitch on a spare piece of the fabric you have chosen. For ordinary seaming and most sewing situations, straight stitch lengths range from 10-15 stitches per 2.5cm (1in). For gathering, the length ranges from 6-9 stitches per 2.5cm (1in). And for seaming lightweight fabrics, use a finer stitch ranging from 16-24 stitches per 2.5cm (1in). Check the tension and adjust, if necessary. The correct tension should show the link formed with each stitch to lie midway between the fabric layers – so the stitching will look the same on both sides of the fabric.

SEAMS

Unless otherwise stated within a project, most seams used throughout the book are plain open seams which are first stitched, trimmed back and then clipped or notched, depending on the location and the type of fabric used.

1 Machine (or hand) stitch the seam, and then trim the seam allowance from 13mm (½in) to 6mm (¼in) or as instructed. The fabric is cut away to reduce bulk, especially necessary for making dolls.

2 Convex or outward curved seams should then be clipped. Cut small slits into the seam allowance. These will spread out and allow the edge to lie flat when finished.

3 Notches are V-shaped wedges which are cut out from concave or inward seams to allow the two edges of the V to come together when the seam is turned through and thus reduce bulk.

All the patterns used within the book have markings that are indispensable to accurate cutting out and the subsequent construction of a project. The markings are defined as follows:

- **Cutting line:** heavy outline on a pattern piece.

- **Seamline:** Indicated by a dashed line usually positioned 13mm (½in) inside the cutting line but it does vary with certain projects.

- **Balance marks:** denoted by straight lines, are also construction points used for accurate joining of pieces and may be used on very small pattern pieces for clarity or on others where there are additional marks that would otherwise be confusing.

- **Centre front, centre back:** indicated by a seamline or foldline clearly labelled with CF or CB. (This notation appears on only some pattern pieces.)
- **Grainline:** straight line ending with arrowheads means "place on straight grain of fabric".

- **Place-on-fold bracket:** grainline marking with directional arrows means the outline should be placed exactly on the folded edge of the fabric.

- **Darts:** broken (stitching) lines meet at a centre point.

THE WORKBASKET

The basic equipment needed for making cloth dolls is simple and inexpensive and can be bought from most needlework and craft stores, if you don't already have the items in your workbasket.

NEEDLES

- **Sharps** (sizes 5-10) are round-eyed and sharp-pointed and are used for all hand sewing with general-purpose sewing thread or tacking cotton.
- **Crewel** needles (sizes 1-10) have sharp points and long oval eyes and are used for all forms of fine to medium-weight embroidery using either six-stranded embroidery thread or single threads, such as coton à broder and pearl threads.
- **Chenille** needles (sizes 18-24) are similar to crewel needles but are much bigger and stronger.

- **Bodkin** (usually one size) This is a large oval-eyed round-ended needle useful for working with coarse yarns and fabrics.
- **Elastic threader** (usually one size) is a flat, large-eyed needle with a round point used for threading elastic or narrow ribbon or tape through a casing.

THREADS

- **General-purpose sewing threads** are available in cotton or cotton/polyester. They are produced in a wide range of colours, and it should be possible to match any fabric.

- **Strong thread** or button-hole thread is a tightly twisted single thread with a lustrous finish. It is useful for stitching doll joints that require a flexible shank, for example.
- **Six-stranded embroidery thread** is a loosely-twisted mercerized cotton used for surface embroidery. Produced in a vast array of colours, it can be split and used in varying thicknesses to give lighter or more solid effects.
- **Coton à broder** is a lightly twisted single thread available in a range of colours.
- **Pearl cotton** is a tightly twisted single thread available in a variety of thicknesses and colours.
- **Tacking thread** is a loosely twisted cotton thread (usually white) used for the stitching which temporarily holds together fabric layers.
- **Shirring elastic** or elastic thread: Nylon/cotton wrapped thread. Stretchy and reasonably thick, it is used for shirring on the sewing machine, and is wound on to the bobbin only.
- **Scissors** It is useful to have a pair of dressmaker's shears for cutting fabric; a pair of sharp-pointed embroidery scissors for snipping into seams and a pair of general purpose scissors for cutting paper.

- **Sewing machine** A sewing machine is useful for making up items, especially on larger projects where it will give a stronger seam and quicker results.

- **Knitting needle** A strong knitting needle is the perfect tool for helping to stuff cloth dolls. Use the blunt end for pushing in the stuffing and use the pointed end carefully for getting into corners.
- **Fray check** is a quick-drying sealant that can be applied to the raw edges of fabric to stop them fraying.
- **Dressmaker's carbon paper** is usually sold in packs of different colours. The darker tones are used to transfer marks or motifs to light-coloured fabrics, while lighter shades are used for darker-coloured fabrics.
- **Tracing wheel,** in appearance rather like a pastry wheel, this wheeled marking gauge enables the speedy transition of pattern marks to fabric.
- **Air-vanishing pencil,** as its name implies, is a marking pencil with a temporary effect as the marks will disappear after a short while.
- **Additional items include:** a thermostatically controlled steam iron – ideal for this type of craftwork; fine, stainless steel dressmaker's pins; a thimble; tape measure; ruler and pencil; fabric adhesive.

TYPES OF BODY

Cloth dolls fall into certain categories according to the type of body they have. Some small dolls, for example, are made from just two pieces of fabric while others are made from several; some are flat and others are well-rounded.

There are dolls with fixed limbs and neck like the Pocket Dolls on page 14, which are eminently suitable for the tiny hands of babies and small children. Others, such as the Amish Dolls, page 46, have stitched joints which makes them semi-flexible and can be dressed and undressed more easily. Some of the bigger dolls have shank joints or bead joints, see pages 86 and 118, which allow their limbs to swing easily. Other features such as angled and straight-stitched leg joints enable dolls to balance when sitting down. The information given in the following pages explains in detail the different features that have been used in the construction of the dolls shown within the book.

the smaller sizes make ideal hand toys for babies and small children made simply from gingham or towelling fabric.

Method Cut out the doll pattern from your chosen fabric allowing a 13mm (½in) seam allowance all round. Machine stitch around leaving an opening at the top of the head. Trim the seam by half, snip into the neck, between the limbs and into the curved seam, and turn through. Lightly stuff so that the doll remains flat but slightly rounded and flexible. Slip stitch the opening to close.

Combined head and body dolls have separate limbs which can be attached with either an angled or straight seam depending on the shape of the body. The body may also be curved at the waist to give a female shape.

around the shape, reinforcing the neck and shoulder seam with a second row of stitching. Clip into the curves and turn through. Stuff to give a soft, flexible finish and slip stitch the opening to close. Attach the limbs by oversewing them to the body, as instructed.

Straight-stitched joints (arms and legs) may be stitched through on a combined body and limb doll to give a little more flexibility, or separate limbs can be inserted or oversewn to the straight sides of the body.

Combined head, body and limbs is the simplest doll construction involving just two sections of fabric cut out in the shape of a doll, see pocket dolls page 14. This type of doll can be any size but

Method Decide on the technique for attaching the limbs of your doll and whether you want a waisted female shape, and then cut out the combined head and body pattern from double fabric. Leaving an opening in the side for turning through, stitch

Method On a combined body and limb doll, simply backstitch the top arm/shoulder and leg joints stitching through all layers. Where individual limbs are attached, make the limbs as instructed and pin them in place to the body. Using strong thread and fairly small stitches, firmly overcast each limb working with the back of the doll uppermost.

Angle-stitched joints give a little more sophistication to the anatomical shape of the doll. Where both the body and limbs are even slightly angled, the limbs will hang naturally downwards but point outwards. Angle-stitched legs will also give the doll a broader base to balance on when sitting down.

Method The technique is generally the same as for straight-stitched joints but some construction methods may leave openings in the body for the stuffed limbs to be inserted and then stitched through all four layers (body and limbs) using backstitch to secure them. In this case, the limbs are left unstitched after stuffing.

Shank joints made by wrapping around several connecting stitches to form a shank, are very strong and offer the most flexibility for both arms and legs. Used mainly on bigger dolls, shank leg joints will enable the doll to sit in a well-balanced position.

Method This is similar to making a button shank. Several connecting threads are taken across from the body to the limb; then the threads are wrapped around to form a shank, finishing off by taking the needle through the body. Use strong thread to ensure a long-lasting joint.

Tubular body forms the lower part of the doll and enables it to stand on a flat circular base in order to display, for example, an ethnic-style costume. The hollow cardboard tube is weighted to help keep the doll upright.

Method A cardboard circular base is first attached to one end of the empty tube. Dried beans, or other suitable fillings, are then put inside and a cardboard lid attached. The tube is then inserted into the fabric body where the head and shoulders have already been stuffed. The lower edge of the fabric is gathered over the bottom of the tube and separate arms oversewn in place to complete the body.

Bead joints are very decorative and also give flexibility to the knee and elbow joints. The size of the beads should be in proportion to the size of the limbs, and the central hole should be big enough to allow the chosen fabric to be threaded through.

Method Choose the colour of bead to complement the fabric of your doll. Beginning with the lower part of the limb (the foot or the hand), stuff firmly, as instructed, as far as the knee or elbow joint and then thread on the bead. Push the bead down firmly and continue stuffing the upper part of the limb. Oversew the opening to close. Attach the arms and legs to the doll's body following the instructions given.

Three-dimensional body and limbs involves stitching together several pattern pieces to make a separate head, body, arms and legs. These are then stuffed firmly, sometimes quite hard, and with a well-rounded finish. The doll is usually assembled with a forward projecting face and feet and with defined fingers.

Method The individual pattern pieces are cut out and stitched in the usual way (the body and upper limbs can be made from a contrasting patterned fabric). The different parts are then stuffed using a knitting needle to push the stuffing well in. To give shape to the face, a dart on the front head section forms the chin. The neck of the stuffed head is inserted into the stuffed body and oversewn around the base of the neck. The legs and arms are pleated at the top edge, placing the seams in the centre, before securing them to the body. This ensures that the feet and the profile of the hands point forward. The fingers are then defined with rows of backstitching.

Double-headed body is used for the Upsidedown Doll, see page 40, where the doll's long skirt is also "double" and hides the second doll when the opposite doll is held in an upright position.

Method The combined pattern of a body with a head at each end (reversed at the waist) is cut out, stitched and stuffed in the usual way. Two sets of arms are also made and are attached at the shoulders with shank joints. The doll has no legs.

FACES AND HAIR

Painted face and eyes

Before a doll is given clothes, its character is firmly established with the addition of the face and hair. Features can vary enormously from a few embroidered lines as on the Rabbit Pocket Doll, page 22, to the multicoloured effect of the Painted doll, page 24.

Hair can be as simple as knotted lengths of raffia, as in the Pyjama-case Doll on page 86, or as elaborate as the Classic Doll's coiffure, page 108. The following information lists the variety of styles and techniques that have been used within the book, but with a little imagination, you can easily combine and adapt these techniques.

FACES

Embroidery usually involves stitching the features directly onto the face with coloured embroidery threads and using a variety of embroidery stitches such as satin and stem stitch.

Method Using either a freehand pencil line or dressmaker's carbon paper, transfer the features from the pattern to the right side of the fabric – ideally before the head is finished. Work the embroidery after stuffing, strengthening any faint lines with a pencil. Begin by inserting the needle

some distance away from the face detail, leaving a short thread hanging. Secure it at the first stitch and trim back later. Do the same in reverse for finishing. (See the stitch glossary).

Appliqué is the technique whereby the features are cut out from non-fraying fabric and applied to the face with fabric adhesive, hemstitching or decorative embroidery stitches.

Method As a guideline, transfer the simple outline of the features to the fabric as for "Embroidery". Cut out the features from a non-fraying fabric like felt, and use fabric adhesive to fix them in place. Shapes can then be hemstitched around using a matching thread and/or decoratively embroidered with coloured threads. Eyes and cheek circles, for example, can be overstitched with contrasting crossed stitches.

Soft sculpture, as its name implies, involves pulling stitches down into the filling to form features on the doll's face.

Method In order to give depth to the features, the face fabric should not be too stiff nor the stuffing too hard. Using an air-vanishing pencil, transfer

guidelines to the face before stitching. With matching, strong (or double) thread in a long needle, insert the needle from the back of the stuffed head, make a small stitch and return the needle to the back pulling the thread tight. Continue in this way until you have the desired feature effect, finishing off at the back underneath the hair.

Painting can include using different coloured fabric paints, fabric dyes or water-soluble crayons to suggest features and hair.

Method Fabric paints and dyes can be watered-down to give varying tones and shades. Practise first on spare fabric with different size brushes, colours and shaded effects. Transfer guidelines, using an air-vanishing pencil, to the stuffed head and paint directly on the fabric. Allow the paint to dry between applications and remember to clean brushes well before mixing new colours.

Waterproof markers and cosmetic blushers: Waterproof markers (available in a variety of colours) can be used successfully to "draw" in the features. Cosmetic blushers are ideal for suggesting a "blush" on the cheeks of a doll.

Plastic safety eyes and drawn-on features

Raffia hair

Bead eyes, embroidered nose and mouth

Soft sculpture face

Appliqued features

Embroidered face and hair

Method Waterproof markers are ideal for suggesting features, either as a simple outline or as a "feathered" line, as in eyebrows, for example. Following a guideline, which can be made with an ordinary or air-vanishing pencil, draw directly onto the stuffed face with the appropriate marker. For a very quick effect, mouths and eyebrows can be suggested with a single line, and nostrils, freckles and even eyes with dots.

Buttons, beads and safety eyes can all be used to create charming faces. Commercially bought toy eyes have a safety device to lock them in place.

Method Buttons and beads can be used for eyes and cheeks. Secure very firmly and do not use on dolls designed as toys for babies or young children. For ready-made toy eyes, follow the manufacturer's instructions.

HAIR

Yarn is available in a great variety of colours and thicknesses from chunky knitting to two-ply crewel embroidery wool. It can be applied to the head in stitched hanks to be plaited or tied in bunches, or applied in tight curls. Shorter strands can be

unravelled for a tousled look. Thick yarn is particularly good for larger dolls.

Method For either long or short hair, the yarn is first cut into lengths, laid over a piece of tape and stitched to it. The tape is then stuck or stitched to the head and the strands are then neatly arranged over the head. Depending on the style, the yarn is stuck under the hairline around the face and around the neckline before finishing in plaits and so on. Additional layers may be applied on top for a fuller effect.

Embroidery threads offer a wide range of colours, thicknesses and textures. They can be mixed in the needle and stitched directly through the fabric on the head. The scale of these threads is especially good for smaller dolls.

Method One of the most attractive styles uses loop stitch. This is worked all over the head to give a short, curly effect. Using stranded or heavy pearl cotton in the needle, (in mixed, random-dyed or a single colour) work two backstitches; allow the first stitch to remain as a loop (its size determining the depth of the hair) and make the second stitch in the same place but pull this one firmly through to secure the loop. The loops can be left as curls or cut.

Rayon tubular cord is beautifully soft and hangs well. It is fairly narrow, less than 2mm (⅛in) across, is available in several colours and can be used in a similar way to yarn.

Method Wind the cord around two individual pieces of card (each one cut to the hair length required: measured from the centre parting). Then stitch the loops at one end to secure them. Slide each set of loops off the card and neatly stitch together the two secured ends. Stitch this to the centre of the doll's head and finish as for yarn.

Raffia is available in a wide range of colours and in several thicknesses. For "hair", choose the wider variety where coverage is a consideration. Although raffia has a delightful appeal, it should not be used on dolls for small children or babies who may put it in their mouths.

Method Cut the raffia into uneven lengths, roughly 13cm (5in) long, depending on the size of the doll, and with a large chenille needle, thread each length through the head fabric. Secure with a reef knot. Continue to cover the head working around the face, over the back of the head and down the neckline. Space the knots about 13mm (½in) apart.

Fabric strips can be given a particularly charming, homespun effect, especially with country-style ginghams, checks and plaids. The fabric is cut into narrow widths and the edges left to fray before the strips are knotted into the doll's head.

Method Strips of fabric about 13mm (½in) wide are cut, or torn, and then shortened into 10cm (4in) lengths (depending on the size of the doll). Using an elastic threader, or large bodkin, thread the strips through the doll's head making the "stitch" about 1cm (⅜in) wide. Tie each length into a reef knot and leave the edges to fray.

Knotted fabric strips for hair

Buttons for eyes

POCKET DOLLS ARE QUICK AND

EASY TO MAKE AND YOU CAN

PERSONALIZE THEM TO SUIT THE

RECIPIENT. USE ONE OF THE

IDEAS HERE OR DEVELOP

YOUR OWN DESIGNS

POCKET DOLLS

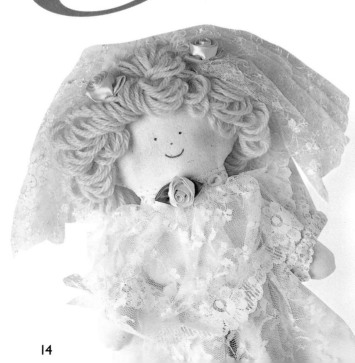

Just two basic pattern pieces are needed to make these versatile pocket dolls. Choose simple flesh-coloured fabric for realistic dolls or let your imagination run riot and use patterned material for unusual, fun effects. Pocket dolls are so simple and inexpensive to make that you can afford to experiment! A washable towelling doll is just right for a baby, while older children will love dolls dressed in their school uniform or sports kit.

MATERIALS

TWIN DOLLS

(measure 24cm (9in) high)

- 46cm (18in) of 90cm (36in) wide lightweight calico for the two bodies
- 10cm (4in) of 25cm (10in) wide fur fabric for the hair
- Polyester filling or kapok
- Waterproof felt-tipped pens (red and black) for the face details
- Pink blusher for the cheeks
- Felt oddments for the eyes
- 23cm (9in) of 90cm (36in) wide printed cotton for the dress and dungarees
- Fabric adhesive
- 36cm (14in) of grosgrain ribbon for boy's braces and bow tie
- Two buttons, about 1cm (⅜in) across, for boy's dungarees
- 46cm (18in) of narrow ribbon for the girl's hair
- 25cm (10in) of round elastic for the dress and dungarees

CHECKED BOY

(measures 24cm (9in) high)

- 30cm × 46cm (12in × 18in) of checked cotton fabric for the body
- 20cm × 30cm (8in × 12in) of contrast cotton fabric for the dungarees
- Oddments of third contrast fabric for the hair
- Polyester filling or kapok
- 25cm (10in) of 1.5cm (⅝in) wide grosgrain ribbon for the braces
- Two small buttons, about 1cm (⅜in) across
- 10cm (4in) of round elastic
- Large eyed chenille needle or bodkin

Fresh cotton prints and trimmings for the twins.

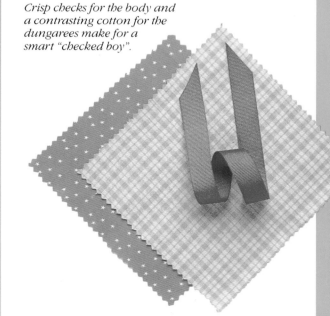

Crisp checks for the body and a contrasting cotton for the dungarees make for a smart "checked boy".

GINGHAM GIRL

(measures 24cm (9in) high)

- 30cm × 46cm (12in × 18in) of brown cotton fabric, such as lawn for body
- Polyester filling or kapok
- 30g (1oz) skein of black wool for the hair
- Oddments of black and red felt for the eyes and mouth
- 46cm (18in) of 6mm (¼in) ribbon for the hair
- 15cm × 41cm (6in × 16in) of checked gingham for the dress
- 15cm (6in) of round elastic for the dress
- Fabric adhesive
- Black waterproof felt-tip pen

RABBIT

(measures 24cm (9in) high)

- 30cm × 46cm (12in × 24in) of blue brushed cotton for the body
- 15cm × 56cm (6in × 22in) of a contrast cotton for the dress and the inner ears
- Oddments of blue felt for the eyes
- Polyester filling or kapok
- Blue stranded embroidery thread for the features
- 15cm (6in) of round elastic
- Fabric adhesive

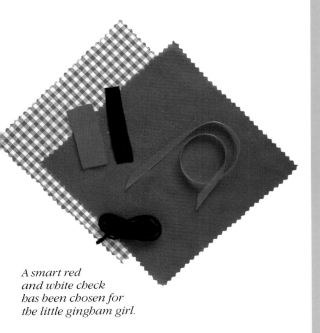

A smart red and white check has been chosen for the little gingham girl.

BRIDE

(measures 24cm (9in) high)

- 30cm × 46cm (12in × 18in) of calico for the body
- 30g (1oz) of wool for the hair
- Polyester filling or kapok
- Fine felt-tipped pens (red and black) and blusher for the face
- 90cm (1yd) of 13cm (5in) wide lace, with one bound edge, for the dress
- 90cm (1yd) of 13cm (5in) wide lace for the veil
- 18cm (7in) of 13mm (½in) wide lace for the collar band
- 46cm (18in) of 1cm (⅜in) wide lace for the wrists
- Three satin ribbon flowers
- 35cm (14in) of round elastic

The bride wears satin rosebuds and different widths of lace.

ANGEL

(measures 24cm (9in) high)

- 30cm × 46cm (12in × 18in) of unbleached calico for the body
- Two blue beads for the eyes
- 25cm (10in) of narrow gold cord for the hair
- 30gm (1oz) of 2mm (⅛in) wide cream nylon knitting ribbon for the hair
- Polyester filling or kapok
- Blue stranded embroidery cotton for the face details
- 25cm × 50cm (10in × 20in) of white cotton fabric for the dress
- 90cm (1yd) of gold trim, such as russia braid, for dress
- 20cm × 30cm (8in × 12in) of white organza for the wings
- Gold sequins to decorate the wings and hair
- 90cm (1yd) of 13mm (½in) wide gold ribbon for the neck and wings
- Six white pipe cleaners for the wings
- Fabric adhesive

A soft brushed cotton body with contrasting spotted cotton for the dress and ears make for a sweet little rabbit. Felt and embroidery thread are used for the facial features.

The pocket angel is made up of scraps of ribbon, gold cord, braid and a star patterned fabric.

DOLL PATTERN PIECES FOR
BASIC DOLL AND DOLL VARIATIONS

- Patterns for this project are life size and do not need to be enlarged. Before pinning on the pattern pieces, see the Checklist opposite.

Leave open

HEAD
AND
BODY

cut 2

HAIR
cut 2

direction
of fur

cutting line for front piece

ANGEL'S
WING

cut 2

RABBIT'S
EAR

cut 2
in main
fabric

cut 2 in
contrast
fabric

Leave open

CHECKLIST

- Trace off the outline of the actual size pattern pieces. Transfer all marks and cut out, see pages 6-7.
- Wash and press the main fabrics to test for shrinkage and colourfastness.
- Cut out the required number for each pattern piece from the correct fabric.
- Set your sewing machine to the required stitch, check the length and tension and do a test run on your chosen fabric, see page 8.
- Seam allowances are included on all the doll body patterns. Stitch and trim back to 6mm (¼in), snip into curved seams and press open, see page 8. Note that individual seam allowances may vary for some of the alternative details such as clothes and the fabric fur hair.

Twin dolls: cutting layout for fur fabric

TWIN DOLLS ~
HEAD AND BODY

1 With the right sides facing, pin, tack and machine stitch around the body leaving the seam open as indicated on the pattern. Trim the seam allowance and snip into the seam at the neck, arms and in between the legs. Turn through to the right side. Stuff evenly, using a large knitting needle to help push the filling in place. Turn in the seam allowance and oversew the opening to close. Make the second doll in exactly the same way.

HAIR

2 For each doll, pin together one front and one back hair piece with the right sides facing and machine stitch around the outer curved edge only. Turn to the right side and glue in place. Cut the boy's hair 6mm (¼in) shorter around the face. Tie the narrow ribbon in a decorative bow and sew to the centre of the girl's hair.

FACE

3 For the eyes, cut four 6mm (¼in) circles from the felt and glue two to each face. Suggest the nose and mouth with fine felt-tipped pens, and the cheeks with a light dusting of blusher.

CLOTHING PATTERN PIECES FOR BASIC CLOTHING AND CLOTHING VARIATIONS

- Patterns for this project are life size and do not need to be enlarged. Tape the two dress pattern pieces together before cutting the fabric. Before pinning on the pattern pieces, see the Checklist on page 19.

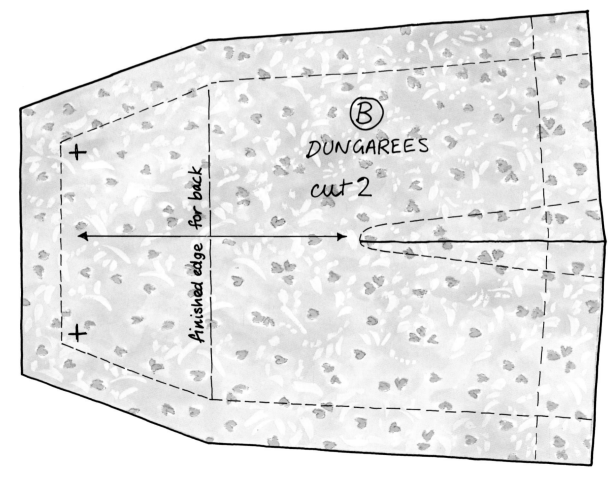

B
DUNGAREES
cut 2

finished edge for back

armhole

Casing for elastic

Join the two dress pattern pieces together before cutting the fabric

leave open

leave open

Ⓐ

DRESS

cut 2

armhole

*Cutting layout for basic
dungarees/trousers and variations*

Cutting layout for basic dress and dress variations

Cutting layout for angel's dress

TWIN GIRL'S DRESS

1 Pin the two dress pieces together with the right sides facing, and machine stitch the side seams from the hem to the notch marked. Press the seam open. Make narrow double turnings on each armhole opening and machine stitch to secure.

2 On the front and back pieces of the dress, make a 13mm (½in) double turning along the neck edge to form a casing. Thread the elastic through both casings to fit the neck and oversew the ends together. Pin and machine stitch a 6mm (¼in) hem along the bottom of the dress to finish.

TWIN BOY'S DUNGAREES

3 On the trouser front piece, pin and machine stitch a narrow hem, first along the side edges and then across the top of the bib, and also along the waistline of the trouser back piece.

4 With the right sides facing, machine stitch the back and front pieces together along the sides and around the inner leg seams. Clip the seam allowance between the legs after sewing. Turn up the leg hems to the required length and hem stitch.

5 From the ribbon, cut two straps each 13cm (5in) long and hand sew them to each side of the front bib on the wrong side. Attach the two small buttons on top. Cross the straps at the back and secure with back stitch just below the stitchline. Thread the elastic through the hem at the back waistline, adjust the length for a correct fit and oversew the ends to hold.

BOY'S BOW TIE

6 Make the bow tie from the remaining ribbon by folding it, as shown, and tightly tying around the centre with sewing thread. Glue or sew it in place on the boy's neck.

CHECKED BOY ~ BODY AND CLOTHES

1 Make the doll from the checked cotton fabric and the dungarees from a contrasting fabric (see the recommended materials list on page 16). Follow step 1, page 19 and steps 3-5, pages 21-22.

HAIR

2 Cut several lengths of fabric about 10cm (4in) long by 1cm (⅜in) wide. With a length of fabric in the chenille needle or bodkin, make a small stitch and pull it through the fabric on top of the doll's head. Tie with a reef knot and repeat at random over the top of the head, as shown.

GINGHAM GIRL ~ BODY AND CLOTHES

1 Following the instructions given on page 19, step 1, make the doll from the brown cotton fabric as suggested (for recommended materials, see page 16).

2 Cut two 1cm (⅜in) circles from the black felt for the eyes and a 1.5cm (⅝in) wide crescent from the red felt for the mouth. Glue these in place and then suggest the nose with a fine felt-tipped pen.

3 For the fringe, cut several 15cm (6in) lengths of wool and tie them together in the centre. Glue this to the top of the head with the cut ends falling forward. Cut the remaining wool into 46cm (18in)

lengths and, again, tie around the centre with a separate length of wool. Glue the centre of the tied strands to the top of the head making the tying strand the centre parting. Glue also around the hairline of the face and neck. Plait the loose strands to the side of the head; cut the ribbon in half and tie around to secure the ends of the plaits. Trim the ends to finish.

4 Make the dress from the checked gingham following the instructions given on page 21, steps 1 and 2.

RABBIT DOLL ~ BODY AND CLOTHES

1 Make the doll and clothes following the materials list on page 16 and the instructions given on page 19, step 1 and page 21, steps 1 and 2. Cut two 6mm (¼in) circles from the blue felt for the eyes and glue them in place. Embroider the nose and whiskers using long straight stitches.

2 Pin the four ear pieces together using one main and one contrast fabric piece for each ear and with right sides facing. Machine stitch around each curved edge. Turn through to the right side. Turn in the seam allowance at the opening and oversew the edges together by hand. Pin the ears in position on top of the head folding the outer edges inwards and hem stitch in place.

BRIDE ~
BODY AND CLOTHES

1 Make the doll from the calico following the materials list on page 17 and the instructions given on page 19, step 1. Draw in the face using the black pen for the nose and suggest the cheeks with a light dusting of blusher.

2 To make the hair cut a long length of wool and wind it around a ruler. Backstitch along the top edge to hold the loops together. Slip the loops off the ruler and hem stitch in place in rows across the head beginning at the base of the neck. Repeat until the head is completely filled. For smaller curls, wind the wool around a pencil.

3 Cut the dress lace in half to make a separate skirt and top. Cut 20cm (8in) of elastic for the waist and 15cm (6in) for the neck. Thread the 20cm (8in) of elastic through the binding on one of the pieces of lace and knot the ends together. Fit this skirt on the doll with a centre back opening. Thread the other piece of elastic through the remaining lace to make the top of the dress. On this piece, join the raw edges together with a line of running stitches and then draw them up to make a finished shoulder width of about 5cm (2in). Repeat on the opposite shoulder.

4 Sew the 13mm (½in) wide lace around the neck by hand and glue one of the flowers to the centre front. Cut the 1cm (⅜in) wide lace in two and tie around each wrist. Gather the unfinished edge of the veil lace by machine and hand sew it to the top of the head in a semicircle and stitch two flowers at each corner.

ANGEL ~
BODY AND CLOTHES

1 Make the doll from the calico following the materials list on page 17 and the instructions given on page 19, step 1.

2 For the hair, wind the knitting ribbon around a piece of card 13cm (5in) deep, dividing it into two separate skeins. Tie each skein firmly around one end, and remove from the card. Oversew the two skeins to the centre of the head so that they fall to each side of the face. Glue down along the hairline and secure with the narrow gold cord around the head. Hold the cord in place by stitching a sequin to the centre parting, as shown. For the eyes, hand sew the two small beads in place and then, using one strand of embroidery thread, make a straight stitch for the nose and a French knot for the mouth.

3 To make the long dress with sleeves, use the white cotton fabric and follow the dress instructions given on page 21, step 1 and 2 but first extend the length of the dress to 17cm (6½in) and, for the sleeves, cut two strips 6.5cm × 13.5cm (2½in × 5¼in) from the same fabric.

4 Using the wing pattern as a template, twist to join three pipe cleaners together and mould to the required shape. Repeat for the second wing. Cut two wings from the organza and glue the pipe cleaners in place. Stick on the sequins to decorate the top half of each wing. Oversew the wings together at the centre point and then stitch them to the centre back of the doll. Tie the remaining 13mm (½in) wide ribbon in a bow and stitch it over the joining.

OTHER POCKET DOLL VARIATIONS

A pocket ballerina made from brown cotton, pink satin and stiffened net.

Green organza, blue satin and shredded paper are used for this charming mermaid.

This pink towelling baby wears a lace-trimmed mob cap.

NO-SEW CLOTHES MAKE THIS

PAINTED DOLL THE IDEAL PROJECT

FOR LESS EXPERIENCED

NEEDLEWORKERS AND FOR

CHILDREN EAGER TO LEND A

HELPING HAND

FABRIC-PAINTED DOLL

Sew and stuff a very simple body, then use fabric paints to create the clothes, face, hair and shoes of your choice. Fabric paints are now available in a very wide range of colours and textures so you will be able to achieve an exciting variety of effects.

Metallic gold and silver paints will produce a stunning Christmas angel for example – or paints with a raised, bead-like texture can be used for unusual jewellery or hair effects.

MATERIALS

DOLL (measures 27cm (10½in) high)

- 40cm × 26cm (16in × 10in) of lightweight unbleached calico for the body
- Loose polyester filling or kapok
- Fabric paints in the colours of your choice (blues, pinks and greens are suitable for traditional garments: browns for hair)
- Paintbrushes in varying sizes (fine to medium)
- Pencil

PANTALOONS

- 26cm × 20cm (10in × 8in) of fine white cotton fabric for the pantaloons
- 30cm (12in) of lace trim

Unbleached calico, fine white cotton and lace trim for the body and clothes.

DOLL PATTERN PIECES

Patterns for this project are life size and do not need to be enlarged. Before pinning on the pattern pieces, see the Checklist opposite.

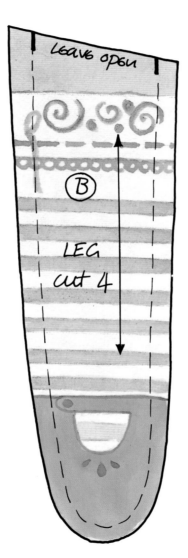

Leave open

B

LEG cut 4

HEAD AND BODY cut 2

A

C

ARM cut 4

Leave open

CHECKLIST

- Trace off the outline of the actual size pattern pieces, transfer all marks and cut out, see pages 6-7.
- Wash and press all main fabrics to test for shrinkage and colourfastness, see page 6.
- Cut out the required number for each pattern piece from the appropriate fabric.
- Set your sewing machine to the correct stitch, length and tension and do a test run on your chosen fabric, see page 8.
- Seam allowances are included and should be stitched and trimmed back to 3mm (⅛in), see page 8.
- Before painting the doll, test the paint on a spare piece of fabric.

Cutting layout for unbleached calico

THE DOLL ~ HEAD AND BODY

1 With the right sides inside, pin, tack and machine stitch the two head and body pieces together leaving a 2.5cm (1in) opening along one side. Double stitch at each side of the neck for extra strength. Remove tacking.

2 Using small scissors, snip into the curved seam allowances just short of the stitching, at the neck, around the head and the waist.

3 Turn through to the right side. Stuff and, using the end of a knitting needle to push the stuffing into the corners, make a smooth, well-padded shape. Turn in the raw edges of the opening and, using matching sewing thread, oversew to close.

ARMS AND LEGS

4 Machine stitch the arm pieces together, in the same way, leaving the short sides open on each arm. Turn to the right side and stuff evenly, as before, making sure you keep the angle as it appears on the pattern so that the arms will point downwards once they are stitched to the body. Using matching thread neatly slip stitch the opening to close. Attach the arms (as shown on the pattern) to the body with small oversewing stitches. Check they are the same length.

5 Repeat in exactly the same way for the legs. You will notice that the legs are similarly angled so they will hang neatly downwards from the body.

HAND PAINTING THE BODY AND FACE

6 Following the colour diagram given on the pattern, begin by marking the basic areas of the undergarments onto the doll with a very light pencil line. Finer details such as bows, dots and buttons can be applied to the basic colours when they have dried. Using a fairly fine brush and adding a little water to the paint, apply the appropriate colours to the knickers and camisole, hands and shoes. Leave the paint to dry thoroughly before adding the finer details such as the lace edgings, buttons and bows. For this, use a very fine brush and not too much water otherwise the paints may bleed into each other.

7 Using a light pencil line, draw in the hairline, eyes, eyebrows, lips, cheeks and necklace, freehand. Paint the eyes first then a line around them to form the shape of the eyes and the eyebrows. Add two dots for the nose and, finally, paint the lips. To achieve the look of delicate eye make-up, water down the paint considerably and apply it carefully to the eyelids. Do the same for the cheeks. Now colour in the hair and, with a steady hand, add little curls around the face. Finish by adding the necklace of multi-coloured beads.

The painted on undergarments continue on the back of the doll.

CLOTHING PATTERN PIECES

- Patterns for this project are life size and
- do not need to be enlarged. Before
- pinning on the pattern pieces, see the
- Checklist on page 27.

Place on fold

Ⓑ

PANTALOON DRAWSTRING cut 1

PANTALOONS

cut 4

Ⓐ

Cutting layout for fine, white cotton fabric

Fold

B

A

28

THE CLOTHES ~
PANTALOONS

1 Place the four pieces together to make two pairs and, with the right sides inside, pin, tack and machine stitch along the curved edges of each pair.

2 Clip into the curved seam and press open. Place the two sections together right sides inside. Tack and machine stitch the inner leg seams in one continuous operation. Machine stitch the side seams and fingerpress the seams open. Remove the tacking stitches.

3 Make narrow double turnings on each leg to neaten and, using matching sewing thread, secure with a row of small running stitches. Repeat on the waist edge but make the turning slightly bigger to allow for the drawstring to be threaded through.

4 Pin the lace trim around the lower edge of each leg and, using matching sewing thread, secure with small running stitches. Overlap the lace edges on the inside leg seam, for neatness.

5 Turn the pantaloons right side out and, using small scissors, make an upright slit in single fabric at the side of the waistband, just big enough for the drawstring to pass through. Neaten the edges of the slit with small buttonhole stitches, working in the same way as for a buttonhole.

6 To make the drawstring, turn under the short ends by 6mm (¼in) and press. Now turn in the long sides until they meet in the middle of the fabric. Fold the fabric lengthways, press and tack to secure. Using matching thread, hand stitch with small running stitches.

7 Attach the short end of the drawstring to a small safety pin and thread it through the waistband, ready to tie into a bow.

YOU CAN CREATE A WHOLE

COLLECTION OF DOLLS WITH

TRADITIONAL COSTUMES

USING THIS QUICK AND

EASY TECHNIQUE

COSTUME DOLLS

The body of this doll has been specially designed for display and is very quick to make. So once you have followed the simple instructions for making the body, you are free to create any number of different dolls.

In particular, this technique is ideal for making a collection of dolls wearing national or traditional costumes. Start by copying the dolls here and then research pictures of other costumes to create your own designs.

Traditional print fabrics with a strong pattern for the dress

MATERIALS

DOLL (measures 24cm (9½in) high)

- 30cm × 46cm (12in × 18in) of brown, lightweight cotton fabric for the doll
- One small ball of brown or black wool for the hair
- One cardboard tube about 12cm (4½in) high for the doll base
- 10cm (4in) square of card, (cereal box card is suitable)
- Sticky tape
- Loose polyester filling or kapok
- Brown, white and red embroidery thread for the facial features
- Small beads for the jewellery
- Dried beans, pulses or pebbles for weighting the base of the doll
- White dressmaker's carbon paper

DRESS

- Two pieces of African-style fabric measuring 30cm × 70cm (12in × 28in) and 26cm × 50cm (10in × 20in)

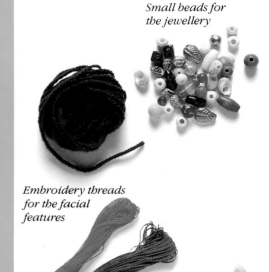

Small beads for the jewellery

Embroidery threads for the facial features

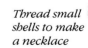

Thread small shells to make a necklace

Alternative fabrics could be chosen

DOLL PATTERN PIECES

- Patterns for this project are life size and do not need to be enlarged. Note pattern pieces for the body and head must be taped together before cutting the fabric. Before pinning on the pattern pieces, see the Checklist overleaf.

Ⓒ

BASE

cut 1

place on fold

Ⓐ

gathering line

HEAD

cut 2

Ⓑ ARM

cut 4

leave open

Ⓐ

BODY

cut 2

leave open

Join head and body pattern pieces together before cutting fabric

CHECKLIST

- Trace off the outline of the actual size pattern pieces, transfer all marks and cut out, see pages 6-7.
- Wash and press all main fabrics to test for shrinkage and colourfastness, see page 6.
- Cut out the required number for each pattern piece.
- Set your sewing machine to the correct stitch, length and tension and do a test run on your chosen fabric, see page 8.
- Seam allowances are included and should be stitched and trimmed back to 3mm (⅛in), see page 8.

The cardboard tube is filled with dried beans to stabilize it.

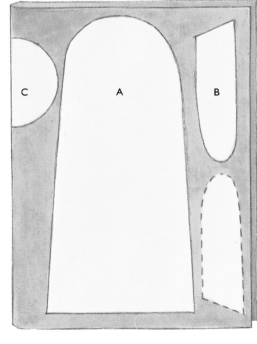

Cutting layout for brown, lightweight cotton fabric

Fold

C   A   B

THE DOLL ~ BODY AND HEAD

1 Place the cardboard tube on the piece of card and draw around its base. Draw a second circle and cut out both pieces. Using sticky tape, attach one circular piece of card to one end of the tube.

2 Fill the tube with dried beans, for example, or small pebbles until it feels fairly sturdy. Then place the other cardboard circle on top and attach it as before. Put the tube to one side.

3 With the right sides inside, place the two head and body pieces together. Pin, tack and machine stitch around, leaving the bottom edge open.

4 Trim the seam to 3mm (⅛in) and, using sharp scissors cut small notches into the curved seam allowance just short of the stitching. Now turn to the right side and lightly press. Before stuffing the head, trace off the facial details given on the pattern piece and, using dressmaker's carbon paper, transfer them to the doll.

5 Use double sewing thread knotted at one end and make a line of gathering stitches all the way around to form the neck, as shown on the pattern piece. Leave a length of sewing thread so that you can rethread it later and gather up the stitches to form the head.

7 Continue to stuff the body to a depth of approximately 8cm (3in) using a knitting needle to help give it a fairly firm finish. This forms the middle of the body. Run a row of gathering stitches along the bottom edge about 1cm (⅜in) in, and leave the thread ungathered.

9 Make tiny snips into the curved seam allowance of the doll base. Turn the seam under and press flat. Pin it to the base of the doll to neaten. With matching thread, neatly oversew around the edge.

ARMS

6 With well-teased-out stuffing, fill the head above the line of stitching until it is quite firm. It may help to use the end of a knitting needle to push the stuffing in firmly. Once you have sufficiently filled the head, rethread your needle with the sewing thread left earlier. Pull the thread firmly so that the fabric is tightly gathered. This forms the neck. Secure with a couple of oversewn stitches.

8 Ease the cardboard tube into the bottom half of the body. Check that there is the right amount of stuffing to form the middle of the body. Then pull the gathering thread tight and oversew to secure so that the tube is held in place. The whole shape should be quite firm, sturdy and straight.

10 With right sides inside, place the four arm pieces together to make two arms. Tack and machine stitch around each arm piece, leaving the short straight sides open ready for turning through. Trim the seams, snip into the curved seam allowance of each arm. Turn them both to the right side and stuff, using the end of a knitting needle to reach into the 'hand'.

11 Turn under the raw edge of the opening and slip stitch to close. Matching the arms to the positioning marks given on the pattern, attach them to the doll using small oversewing stitches.

FACE

12 Using the appropriate colours (two strands in the needle if using stranded threads), embroider the facial details. With the brown thread, work the doll's eyebrows in stem stitch and her eyes in satin stitch. Using white thread outline her eyes and eyelids with backstitches, suggesting eyelashes with four diagonal straight stitches. Continuing with white thread, work the nose in stem stitch. Finish by embroidering the mouth in red with two rows of stem stitch.

HAIR

13 From the ball of wool, cut 72 lengths about 13cm (5in) long (depending on how long you want to make the hair). Divide the wool into twelve sets of six strands and secure each set with a knot at one end.

14 Using matching thread, attach the hair to the head with backstitching. The knots should lie on the seamline on top of the head, with the wool strands falling over the face. Continue to attach all twelve hair pieces in the same way around the edge of the face.

15 Plait each hair piece and secure the ends by tying them around with a length of thread. Then slip stitch each plait to the back of the head, passing the needle through the thickness of the plait, until you reach the back of the neck. The plaits should lie neatly side-by-side, covering the back of the head.

JEWELLERY

16 Decorate the hair by attaching small beads, sequins or tiny shells to each plait, stitching groups of two, three or four mixed colours at the point where the plait was secured with matching thread. Similarly, thread sufficient tiny beads to make a bracelet and necklace. In each case, attach them with one or two oversewing stitches to the back of the wrist and at the back of the neck respectively. Make the necklace long enough to fit just inside the 'V'neck of the dress.

CLOTHING PATTERN PIECES

Patterns for this project are life size and do not need to be enlarged. Before pinning on the pattern pieces, see the Checklist on page 34.

gather

Ⓑ SLEEVE

cut 2

hem line

Ⓐ

BODICE
Front and back

cut 2

Ⓒ cut 2

BODICE FACING
Front and back

Other pattern pieces:

From African-style fabric cut the following rectangles on the straight grain:

Dress skirt Ⓓ 10cm x 37.5cm
(4in x 14¾in)

Upper frill Ⓔ 6.5cm x 61cm
(2½in x 24in)

Lower frill Ⓕ 6.5cm x 67cm
(2½in x 26½in)

COSTUME DOLLS

Cutting layout for African-style fabric: single layer

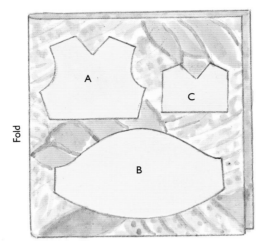

Cutting layout for African-style fabric: folded

3 With the right sides inside, pin, tack and stitch the two bodice pieces together at the shoulder seams and side seams. Press the seams open.

THE CLOTHES ~
DRESS

1 With the right sides inside, place one section of the bodice facing and one of the bodice pieces together, lining up the 'V'neck. Pin, tack and then machine stitch around the 'V'neck. Repeat on the second bodice piece.

2 Snip into the seam allowance, just short of the stitching and turn the facing on both bodice pieces to the wrong side leaving a neat seam along the neckline. Press.

4 With each sleeve, place the underarm seams together, right sides inside, then tack and machine stitch. Press the seams open. Make a line of running stitches along the sleeve head just inside the seam allowance. Gather gently so that the sleeve fits the armhole.

7 Attach the lower frill in the same way as for the upper frill but, this time, align the edge of the frill with the edges of the main skirt. Remove all tacking threads.

5 Insert the sleeve into the armhole, right sides together and, with shoulder seam and balance points matching, pin, tack and either machine stitch or hand sew in place using small back-stitching. Make a small turning on the lower edge of the sleeve, tack and slip stitch.

6 On each frill, begin by machine stitching a narrow double turning along one long edge. For the upper frill, pleat the raw edge with 6mm (¼in) wide pleats spaced about 2.5cm (1in) apart. Pin, tack and machine stitch to hold. With right sides together, place the pleated frill, as shown in the diagram, about 2.5cm (1in) from the waist edge of the main skirt. Make sure the short edges of the frill overlap the main skirt by 6mm (¼in). Pin, tack and machine stitch in place.

8 With right sides inside, place the two short edges of the upper frill together and machine stitch. With the skirt right sides together, tack and machine stitch along the skirt and the lower frill in one continuous seam. Stitch above the top frill. Lightly press the frills so that they lie correctly.

9 Gather the top of the skirt, on a line just inside the seam allowance, and pull up the thread so that the skirt waist fits the bodice. With right sides inside, pin, tack and machine stitch the skirt and bodice together. Neaten the seams and turn through to the right side.

HEADSCARF

10 As an alternative to the plaited hair, you may wish to make a headscarf for your doll from a square of leftover fabric and simply knot it in front or behind her head.

ASLEEP OR AWAKE? THE SURPRISING UPSIDEDOWN DOLL CHANGES HER

EXPRESSION TO BE BOTH A DAYTIME TOY AND THE IDEAL DOLL FOR

CHILDREN TO CUDDLE UP WITH AT NIGHT

UPSIDEDOWN DOLL

Bold, bright colours for daytime wear and more subdued patterns for her night attire make the intriguing upsidedown doll a beautiful toy whichever way up she is!

The doll has two heads – one with a wide-awake daytime expression and the other with the eyes closed for the night. Two skirts, joined at the waist, give the doll two different outfits and can be pulled up or down to reveal the appropriate face.

The daytime doll has her hair in bunches, while the night-time doll has a little matching mob cap. Take care with the embroidered faces and you will create a toy to treasure.

MATERIALS

DOLL (measures 50cm (20in) high)

- 46cm (18in) of 90cm (36in) wide lightweight, unbleached calico for the body
- Polyester filling or kapok
- 100g (2oz) of chunky knitting yarn for the hair
- 90cm (1yd) of 1.5cm (5/8in) wide ribbon for the hair
- 68cm (27in) of 150cm (59in) wide cotton fabric for the day dress
- 68cm (27in) of 150cm (59in) wide contrast cotton fabric for the nightdress and mob cap
- 30cm (12in) square of cotton fabric for the mob cap lining
- 46cm (18in) of 2.5cm (1in) wide lace trim for the day dress
- 46cm (18in) of 4cm (1½in) wide lace trim for the nightdress neck
- 1.4m (1½yds) of 2cm (¾in) wide pre-gathered lace trim for the nightdress sleeves and mob cap
- 90cm (1yd) of 4mm (⅛in) wide ribbon to trim the nightdress
- 1.8m (2yds) of 13mm (½in) wide ribbon for both dress belts
- Stranded embroidery cotton in black, red and blue for the facial details
- Shirring elastic
- Fabric adhesive

DOLL PATTERN PIECES

- Patterns for this project should be enlarged to twice the size. If you have access to a photocopier with an enlarging facility set it to 200%. Otherwise trace off the patterns on to a grid, following the procedure outlined on page 7. (See also the Checklist on the opposite page).

Neck trim

Unbleached calico for the body

Contrasting cotton fabric for the day and night dress

Chunky yarn for the hair

Cutting layout for unbleached calico

CHECKLIST

- Enlarge the pattern pieces. Transfer all marks and cut out, see pages 6-7.
- Wash and press the main fabrics, see page 6.
- Cut out the required number for each pattern piece from the appropriate fabric, see page 7.
- Set your sewing machine to the correct stitch, length and tension and do a test run on your chosen fabric, see page 8.
- Seam allowances are included throughout. Unless otherwise stated, stitch and trim back to 6mm (¼in), snip into the curved seams and press open, see page 8.

THE DOLL ~ BODY

Note: before stitching the body section together, you will find it helpful to trace off the facial details and transfer them to the calico using dressmaker's carbon paper.

1 With the two calico pieces right sides facing, machine stitch around the body leaving an opening down one side, as indicated on the pattern. Clip into the curved seam allowances and turn through to the right side. Press. Insert the filling using a knitting needle to push the stuffing in evenly. Oversew the edges of the opening to close.

2 Make two pairs of arms in the same way and then sew them to the body aligning them with the points as marked on the pattern. With double

thread in the needle, make three or four stitches, as shown in the diagram, stitching through the same places in the body and arm for neatness and for added strength.

3 Wrap the sewing thread around the stitches between the body and arms to form a shank so that the arms can swing freely. Take the wrapping thread back through the arm and secure within the holding threads.

4 Outline the fingers with backstitch along the lines shown. Using matching thread, make sure the beginning and ending of the stitching is secure. Pull the stitching firmly to give form to the fingers.

SLEEPING DOLL'S HAIR

5 To make a fringe, cut about 20 lengths of yarn 30cm (12in) long and anchor the ends of the yarn to the top of the head with one or two backstitches, allowing the yarn to fall forward over the face. Backstitch the strands to the head along the fringe line and then fold them back again where they can be stitched in place to the top of the head and also along the neckline.

6 Cut sufficient 23cm (9in) lengths of yarn to make a hank which, when tied in the middle and placed on top of the head, will fully cover the area from the hairline on the face to the back of the head covering the yarn previously brought over from the fringe. Glue or backstitch onto the head.

HEAD AND BODY

cut 2

leave open

Ⓐ

7 For the remaining hair, wind lengths of yarn around a ruler and secure each loop with a line of backstitch. Slip the loops off the ruler and backstitch or glue them in place along the neckline covering the existing ends of yarn. Repeat as necessary until the neckline is covered.

WAKING DOLL'S HAIR

8 Make the fringe in the same way as for the sleeping doll (see step 5). For the remaining hair, cut sufficient 40cm (16in) lengths of yarn to make a hank which, when tied in the middle and placed on top (centre) of the head, will cover the area from the hairline on the face to the back of the head. Separate the yarn to each side and then glue or backstitch into place along the back neckline. Tie the bunches at each side with ribbon bows and trim the ends if necessary.

FACES

9 Using the appropriate colours, embroider the features as shown on the pattern. Work the eyebrows and eye outlines in stem stitch, using three strands of black thread. Fill in the mouth with stem stitch using three strands of red thread. Work the pupils in satin stitch using three strands of black, and the irises in buttonhole stitch with three strands of blue. Suggest the nose with two French knots using two strands of black thread.

CLOTHING PATTERN PIECES

Patterns for this project should be enlarged to twice the size. If you have access to a photocopier with an enlarging facility set it to 200%. Otherwise trace off the patterns on to a grid, following the procedure outlined on page 7. (See also the Checklist on page 43).

Stitching line for sleeve elastic on nightdress

hemline of nightdress

hemline of day dress

DRESS BODICE AND SLEEVE

cut 2 in each fabric

CF + CB

place on fold

Ⓐ

Other pattern pieces:

For the mob cap Ⓑ, cut out one circle 28cm (11ins) in diameter from the nightdress fabric, and a second circle from plain fabric for the lining.

For the dress skirts Ⓒ, cut two rectangles, each 33cm x 90cm (13in x 36in), one from day-dress fabric and one from nightdress fabric.

Cutting layout for white patterned fabric and yellow patterned fabric

THE CLOTHES ~ SKIRT

1 With the right sides facing, machine stitch each skirt piece separately along the short edge, and press the seams open. Pin and machine stitch both pieces together, right sides inside, along the hem edge, then turn to the right side and press. Using a long machine stitch, make a line of gathering stitches around each waistline. Pull up the gathers until each skirt waist fits around the waistline of the doll. Pin and backstitch to secure.

NIGHTDRESS BODICE

2 Make a single turning on each sleeve edge and cover with broderie anglaise trim. Machine stitch. Using elastic thread on the machine spool and a long machine stitch sew 12mm (½in) in from the hem to form the elasticated cuff. With the right sides facing, machine stitch the back and front bodice pieces together along the sleeve and side.

3 With the right side outside, fit the bodice onto the doll. Turn under the seam allowance at the waistline and hemstitch in place. Turn in the seam allowance at the neck and oversew for about 2.5cm (1in) along each shoulder line.

4 Gather the 4cm (1½in) wide lace to fit around the neck. Turn in one raw edge and overlap to neaten, then hemstitch by hand. Tie the narrow ribbon around the wrists in bows and finish with a third bow stitched to the centre front neck. Tie 90cm (1yd) of the 12mm (½in) wide ribbon around the waist.

MOB CAP

5 With right sides facing, machine stitch around the edge taking a 6mm (¼in) seam allowance and leaving a 5cm (2in) opening for turning to the right side. Clip the seam allowance, turn through and slip stitch the opening to close. Press. Pin and machine stitch the broderie anglaise trim to the edge. Using elastic thread make a line of gathering stitches 2.5cm (1in) from the edge of the circle as for the nightdress sleeves.

DAY DRESS BODICE

6 Make a line of running stitches as shown on the sleeve hem and trim to within 6mm (¼in) of the stitching. With the right sides facing, machine stitch the back and front bodice sections together along the sleeve and side seam in a continuous line. Continue as for step 3.

7 Cut the required lengths of 2.5cm (1in) wide trim to fit around the hem of the sleeves and the neck of the dress. Turn under the raw edge, pin in place and, with matching thread, hemstitch to secure. Tie 90cm (1yd) of 12mm (½in) wide ribbon around the waist and finish in a bow.

TRADITIONAL, FACELESS AMISH-

STYLE DOLLS ARE EASY TO MAKE

AND A CHARMING REMINDER OF

SIMPLER AND QUIETER TIMES

AMISH-STYLE DOLLS

Traditional Amish dolls are not given faces in keeping with the biblical commandment forbidding graven images. Usually dressed in plain greens, blues and purples, we have chosen more upbeat checks and stripes for our dolls.

There are only two pieces – the effect of separate arms and legs is given by easing the stuffing away from the joints and sewing across them. Using fabric paint for the hair and shoes helps keep the overall effect simple and in keeping with their Amish origins.

MATERIALS

DOLLS (measure 29cm (11½in) high)

- 20cm × 36cm (8in × 14in) of lightweight, unbleached calico for each doll
- Polyester filling or kapok
- Black fabric paint for the boy's shoes and hair
- Brown fabric paint for the girl's hair
- Deep blue fabric paint for the girl's shoes
- Fine paint brush

BOY'S CLOTHES

- 25cm × 29cm (10in × 11½in) of lightweight, fine striped cotton for the shirt
- 17cm × 38cm (6½in × 15in) of lightweight denim for the dungarees
- 13cm (5in) square of black felt for the hat

GIRL'S CLOTHES

- 24cm × 35cm (9½in × 14in) of blue and white striped cotton fabric for the blouse
- 23cm × 50cm (9in × 20in) of a small checked cotton fabric for the skirt
- 17cm × 23cm (6½in × 9in) of fine white cotton fabric for the apron
- 13cm × 15cm (5in × 6in) of plain white cotton fabric for the bonnet
- 20cm (8in) of 1cm (⅜in) wide lace trim for the bonnet ties
- Sprigs of lavender for the pocket

Denim and striped cotton for the boy's clothes

Light cotton for the apron and bonnet

Blue and white striped cotton and red check for the girl's clothes

Right leg

Left leg

Join both legs to body before cutting fabric

Calico for the dolls' bodies

DOLL PATTERN PIECES

Patterns for this project are life size and do not need to be enlarged. Note left- and right-leg pieces must be joined to the body piece before cutting the fabric. Before pinning on the pattern pieces, see the Checklist on page 50. Details for the girl doll are shown overleaf.

join right leg

join left leg

HEAD AND BODY

cut 2

leave open

Female hairline

For the girl doll, trace off the shoe and hairline details and transfer them to the boy's body.

Female right foot

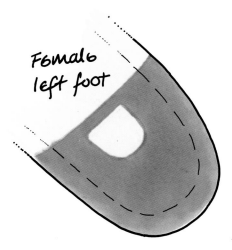

Female left foot

CHECKLIST

- Trace off the outline of the actual size pattern pieces, transfer all marks and cut out, see pages 6-7.
- Wash and press all main fabrics to test for shrinkage and colourfastness, see page 6.
- Cut out the required number for each pattern piece from the appropriate fabric.
- Set your sewing machine to the correct stitch, length and tension and do a test run on your chosen fabric, see page 8.
- Seam allowances are included and should be stitched and trimmed back to 3mm (⅛in), see page 8.

THE DOLL ~ BODY AND HEAD

1 Pin the two body pieces together, right sides facing, and machine stitch around the edge taking a 6mm (¼in) seam and leaving an opening along one side, as shown on the pattern.

2 On a doll like this with fixed arms and legs and of a size that demands narrow seams, it is a good idea to double sew around the underarms, the neck and between the legs for extra strength.

3 Using small scissors, carefully snip into the angled seams, as shown on the pattern, and around the curved seams being careful not to snip into the stitches. Turn the doll to the right side, carefully pushing out the limbs and head with the help of a knitting needle. Press.

4 Using well-teased-out stuffing, begin to stuff the doll starting with the head. Then stuff the arms and the legs and the body last of all. Use the end of a knitting needle to get the stuffing right into the corners evenly and firmly.

CLOTHING PATTERN PIECES
FOR BOY

- Patterns for this project are life size and
- do not need to be enlarged. The shirt
- pieces are shown overleaf. Before pinning
- on the pattern pieces, see the Checklist
- opposite.

HAT BRIM
cut 1
C

D
HAT TOP
cut 1

E
HAT BAND
cut 1

B
BRACES
cut 2

A
attach braces
TROUSERS
cut 4

5 Turn in the raw edges of the opening and, with double thread in the needle, neatly oversew to close. Sew a line of stitches along the tops of the legs and arms stitching through all layers. This will allow the doll's limbs to bend slightly.

6 Working freehand with a light pencil, draw the appropriate male or female shape of the shoes and the hairline onto the doll. Colour them in with the fabric paint (following the manufacturer's instructions) and leave to dry.

attach ties

G
SHIRT FRONT
cut 2

F
SHIRT BACK
cut 1

H
SHIRT SLEEVE
cut 2

gather

J
fold line
TIE cut 2

Cutting layout for striped cotton

Fold

H

F

G

J

Cutting layout for lightweight denim

Fold

B

A

52

BOY'S CLOTHES ~ SHIRT

1 With the right sides facing, pin together the two shirt fronts to the back shirt piece. Machine stitch taking 6mm (¼in) seams. Press the seams open.

2 In the same way, stitch the sleeve seams together and press them open. Lightly gather the sleeve head and pin the sleeves into the armholes, gently easing the fullness to the top of the sleeve. Hand stitch the sleeve in place with small backstitches.

3 Making the tiniest double turnings, neaten the raw edges by hand at the sleeve wrists, along the neckline, around the bottom edge and down the front edges using matching thread and neat running stitches. Press on the wrong side.

4 To make the ties for the shirt, fold in the two long edges so that they meet in the middle and then fold in half. Stitch along the length with running stitches, turn under each end and secure with one or two oversewing stitches. Attach the ties to the neck edge of the shirt front with oversewing stitches.

DUNGAREES

5 Place the four trouser leg pieces together to make two pairs. With the right sides facing, pin and machine stitch around the crotch seam. Clip into the curved seam allowance and press open. Open out the two leg pieces and, with right sides inside,

pin and machine stitch around the inside leg seams in one continuous movement. Stitch the two outside leg seams and press all seams open.

6 To neaten the raw edges along the top and bottoms of the trousers, make narrow double turnings and secure with running stitch.

7 Make the braces in a similar way to the shirt ties, stitching along the length of each one with a row of running stitches. Attach the braces to the front and back of the dungarees on the inside waist edge, neatly oversewing to secure. Cross the braces at the back to give an authentic touch.

53

HAT

Note: as felt is a bonded fabric, care should be taken when handling, especially with some lightweight varieties. Do not, for example, pull knots through as they may tear the felt with disastrous results.

8 Pin the two short sides of the hat band together and, using tiny running stitches, join to form a circle.

9 Fit the top piece into the circular band and join the two edges together. Working with the top uppermost, stitch through both thicknesses pulling the thread fairly firmly to give the finished seam a good shape.

10 In the same way, attach the hat brim to the hat working with the brim uppermost. Trim the seams, if necessary, and turn through to the right side.

CLOTHING PATTERN PIECES
FOR GIRL

- Patterns for this project are life size and
- do not need to be enlarged. Before
- pinning on the pattern pieces, see the
- Checklist on page 50.

(L) BONNET BACK cut 1 — gather

(M) BONNET NECK FACING cut 1

pleats (K) BONNET FRONT cut 1 pleats

gather

(C) BLOUSE SLEEVE cut 2

(B) BLOUSE BACK cut 2

fold here (D) BLOUSE TIE cut 2

SKIRT WAISTBAND   E

fold line

cut 1

H APRON POCKET cut 1

Other pattern pieces:

From the small checked fabric, cut a rectangle on the straight-grain for the skirt N, 16.5cm x 46cm (6½in x 18in)

fold line   SKIRT TIE   cut 2   F

gather

G

A

BLOUSE FRONT

cut 1

APRON cut 1

fold line   J   APRON WAISTBAND/TIE   cut 1

Cutting layout for blue and white striped cotton

Cutting layout for white cotton fabric

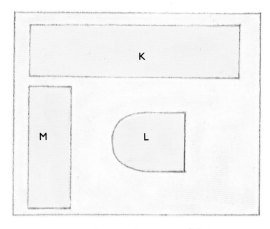

Cutting layout for cotton fabric

GIRL'S CLOTHES ~
SKIRT

1 Make a line of gathering stitches along the top edge of the skirt, just inside the seam allowance. Pull up the thread until the waist edge is just longer than the waistband by 1cm (⅜in).

2 With the right sides inside, pin the two short sides of the skirt together and machine stitch to within 4cm (1½in) of the waist edge. Press open. Neaten the opening by hemming a narrow double turning on both sides.

3 Pin the waistband to the gathered edge of the skirt, with the right sides together and the seam allowances extending at each side. Machine stitch in place taking a 1cm (⅜in) seam. Turn in the two short edges of the waistband and press the fold.

4 Fold the waistband over to the wrong side, turn under the raw edge and hand stitch to secure.

5 To make the ties for the skirt, first press a single turning on the two short edges, then fold the two long edges in so that they meet in the middle. Fold in half and then hand stitch along the length of the tie using tiny running stitches. Make the second tie and oversew in place to each side of the opening on the inside of the waistband.

BLOUSE

6 Begin by making the two darts on the blouse front. Pin and either machine stitch or backstitch to secure. Press the darts towards the centre front.

7 With the right sides facing, pin the two blouse back sections to the blouse front piece. Machine stitch the two side seams and shoulder seams and press them open.

8 Make a line of running stitches around the sleeve head and lightly gather to fit the armhole. With right sides facing, stitch the sleeve seams together. Pin the sleeves into the armhole also with the right sides facing. Even out the gathers and line up the underarm seam with the side seam of the blouse. Backstitch in place.

9 Making the tiniest double turnings, neaten the bottom of the sleeves, around the neck, the back opening and around the bottom edge of the blouse using small running stitches.

10 Make up the ties as for the boy's shirt. Stitch in place to each side of the back opening inside the neck edge, oversewing to secure.

APRON

11 Begin by machine stitching double turnings on the two side edges of the apron, and then the bottom edge. Neaten the pocket by making single turnings around three sides, and stitching a double turning on the top edge. Attach the pocket to the centre of the apron, as shown on the pattern, leaving the top edge open.

12 Pleat the top edge of the apron with 6mm (¼in) deep pleats until it measures 6cm (2½in) across. Pin and tack the pleats in place. With right sides together, pin the waistband/tie centrally over the apron with edges matching and stitch across.

13 Turn in the two short edges. Fold the waistband tie to the wrong side, turn under the seam allowance and hand stitch across the entire length using small running stitches.

BONNET

14 Make a line of running stitches along one long edge of the main bonnet piece. Pull up the thread so that the gathered edge fits around the back bonnet section. With right sides together, pin and hand stitch the two pieces together, stitching with the back section uppermost.

15 Neaten the front edge of the bonnet, with the tiniest double turning secured with running stitches. Make three small pleats at each side to help shape the bonnet, and neatly oversew in place. Gather the neck edge of the bonnet until the edge is the same length as the neck facing.

16 With right sides together, pin the neck facing to the bonnet and stitch across. Fold in the two short edges of the neck facing, make a single turning on the long edge and hand stitch to the inside of the bonnet. Oversew the ends to neaten and attach the lace ties to each side.

There is something very appealing about well-worn and therefore well-loved toys. If you haven't been lucky enough to inherit any antique cloth dolls it is very easy to create your own – either for display or as very unusual and charming gifts. These dolls hark back to the days when, if there was time to make toys, they would be made from any odd, leftover scraps. So don't spend a lot of money on fabric or hair. See what you have lying around at home. Perhaps some out-grown children's clothes will make a body or an old dress could be used to furnish buttons for the eyes. Remember that a slightly lopsided body and big stitches are part of the charm of these dolls.

IMAGINE YOU HAVE BEEN

EXPLORING IN GREAT GRANDMA'S

ATTIC - THESE ARE JUST THE SORT

OF TOYS YOU WOULD BE

THRILLED TO FIND TUCKED

AWAY THERE

*A*TTIC

DOLLS

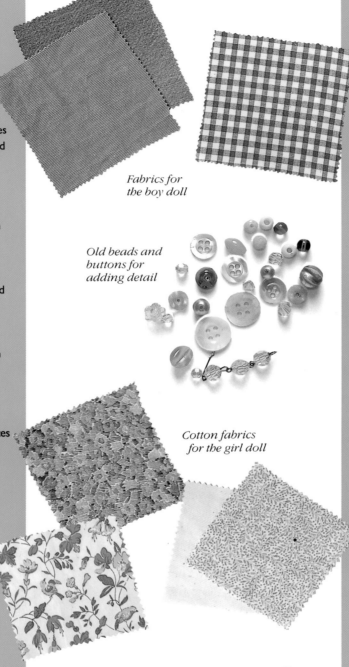

MATERIALS

BOY DOLL (measures 35cm (14in) high)

- 28cm × 56cm (11in × 22in) of light brown needlecord
- Polyester filling or kapok
- Two odd buttons about 13mm (½in) across for eyes
- Embroidery thread in red for the facial details and in brown, black, beige for the hair

JEANS AND HAT

- 32cm × 50cm (12in × 20in) of old blue denim
- 4cm × 4cm (1½in × 1½in) of contrasting cotton fabric for the knee patch

SHIRT

- 27cm × 38cm (10in × 15in) of gingham or checked fabric
- Two old pearl buttons about 1cm (⅜in) across
- Two press studs
- 4cm × 4cm (1½in × 1½in) of contrasting cotton fabric for the patch

BOOTS

- 17cm (6in) square of black felt
- Light coloured thick embroidery thread for the laces

Fabrics for the boy doll

Old beads and buttons for adding detail

Cotton fabrics for the girl doll

MATERIALS

GIRL DOLL (measure 30cm (12in) high)

- 30cm × 48cm (12in × 19in) cream medium weight cotton or calico for the doll
- Polyester filling or kapok
- Stranded embroidery threads in brown and blue for the hair and face; green embroidery thread for the shoes
- Fabric paints in brown, blue and red for the face and hair
- Fine paintbrush and pencil
- Cold tea
- Two old pearl buttons approx 8mm (⁵⁄₁₆in) across

DRESS

- 28cm × 33cm (11in × 13in) of old floral cotton fabric, such as lawn
- 30cm (12in) of 2.5cm (1in) wide old straight-edged lace for the hem
- 15cm (6in) of 13mm (½in) wide old lace for the neck
- Old fabric trimming such as a silk or lace flower

PANTALOONS

- 19cm × 36cm (7½in × 14in) of old contrast floral fabric
- 15cm (6in) of 2cm (¾in) wide old lace

HAT

- 25cm × 30cm (10in × 12in) of contrast floral fabric
- 23cm (9in) of 1cm (⅜in) wide ribbon
- 30cm (12in) of old 13mm (½in) wide lace trim
- Old buttons or small fabric flowers

A selection of lace trims

PATTERN PIECES FOR BOY DOLL

- Patterns for this project are life size and do not need to be enlarged. Before pinning on the pattern pieces, see the Checklist overleaf.

Leave open

Ⓔ
LEFT LEG
cut 2

Leave open

Ⓓ
RIGHT LEG
cut 2

Leave open

Ⓒ
ARM
cut 4

Ⓐ
BODY
cut 2

Leave open

Ⓑ
HEAD
cut 2

Leave open

CHECKLIST

- Trace off the outline of the actual size pattern pieces, transfer all marks and cut out, see pages 6-7.
- Wash and press all fabrics to test for shrinkage. "Antique" both the doll fabric and the clothes fabric, see page 6.
- Cut out the required number for each pattern piece from the appropriate fabric.
- Set your sewing machine to the correct stitch, length and tension and do a test run on your chosen fabric, see page 8.
- Seam allowances are included and should be stitched and trimmed back to 3mm (⅛in), see page 8.

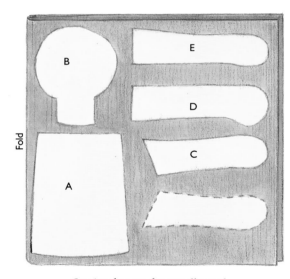

Cutting layout for needlecord

BOY DOLL ~ HEAD AND ARMS

Note: in order to give the boy attic doll an authentic homemade look, it would be better to hand stitch the doll throughout, taking particular notice of the uneven legs and oddly shaped feet and hands, and so on.

1 Pin the two head pieces right sides together and backstitch around, leaving the neck open. Snip into the neck angle and around the curved seam before turning through to the right side. Stuff evenly to give a smooth shape. Pin the neck edges together and put to one side.

2 Backstitch the arm pieces together, snip into the curved seams, turn through and stuff in a similar way. Use the end of a knitting needle to push the stuffing neatly into the shape.

BODY AND LEGS

3 With the right sides facing, pin the two body sections together and backstitch across the shoulders and down the side seams leaving the neck, armholes and bottom edge open.

4 In the same way, stitch the two legs together, turn through and stuff. Pin the raw edges together and put to one side.

ASSEMBLING THE DOLL

5 Turn in the neck edge of the unstuffed body and insert the neck of the stuffed head into the opening. Pin and, with matching thread, hand stitch around the neck working extra stitches at the shoulder seam for extra strength.

Loops of black, brown and beige embroidery thread are used for the hair.

6 Insert the arms at an angle so that they point downwards and stitch in place. This time, with reduced padding in the tops of the arms, use backstitch through all layers pulling the stitches firmly to make the 'joint' more flexible.

7 Now stuff the body to give a soft, evenly shaped finish. Pin the legs in position and stitch across in the same way as for the arms.

HAIR

8 Using the appropriate embroidery threads (black, brown, beige) work the hair as for the memory doll, see page 77. Work with two strands in the needle beginning with the brown thread. Add the black to create density and then work the beige loops for a highlighted effect. Continue to do this until the head is completely covered and the hairline around the face is well-defined.

FACE AND FINGERS

9 Attach two old buttons for the eyes. Using red embroidery thread, suggest the mouth with stem stitch and the cheeks with stars made by crossing simple straight stitches. Apply the fingers to the hands with five straight stitches worked in brown embroidery thread.

CLOTHING PATTERN PIECES
FOR BOY

Patterns for this project are life size and do not need to be enlarged. Before pinning on the pattern pieces, see the Checklist on page opposite.

Ⓐ JEANS cut 4

Ⓑ LEFT SHOE cut 2

Ⓒ RIGHT SHOE cut 2

gather

F

SHIRT SLEEVE

cut 2

E

SHIRT
FRONT

cut 2

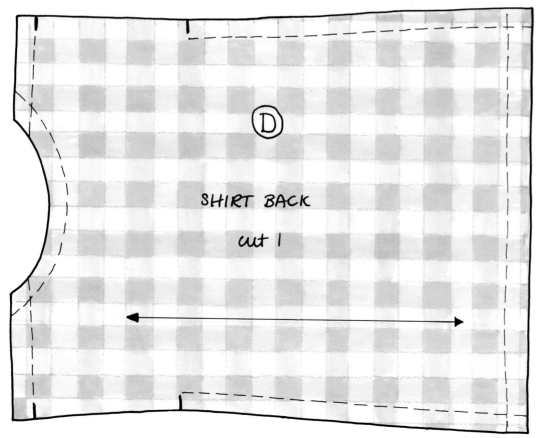

D

SHIRT BACK

cut 1

Other pattern pieces:
For the hat, make paper patterns as follows and cut out of denim fabric.

For the brim Ⓖ, draw a circle 13cm (5in) across with an inner circle 4cm (1½in) across and cut out the inner circle.

For the hat top Ⓗ, cut out another circle 6.5cm (2½in) across.

For the hat band Ⓙ cut out a rectangle 21cm x 5cm (8¼in x 2in)

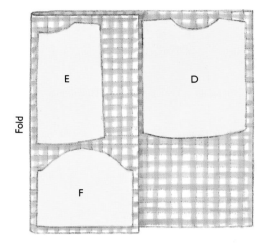

Cutting layout for small check fabric

Cutting layout for old blue denim fabric

BOY'S CLOTHES ~ SHIRT

1 With the right sides together, pin the two shirt front pieces to the shirt back. Backstitch along the shoulder seams and side seams taking a 6mm (¼in) seam.

2 In the same way, join the two sleeve pieces together, and hand stitch along each underarm.

3 With the right sides together, pin the sleeves into the armholes of the shirt easing the fullness of the sleevehead to the top and back of the armhole, and aligning the underarm seams with the side seams. Backstitch in place.

4 Make narrow double turnings around the neckline, the bottom of the shirt and along both shirt fronts and then, with a contrast thread, secure with running stitches of random length. Leave the bottom raw edge of the sleeves unstitched.

5 Attach the two press studs to the front of the shirt. Sew the two odd buttons on top of the press studs on the right side of the shirt. Stitch a little square of contrast fabric to the arm of the shirt, to resemble a patch. Use a contrast thread and large stitches for a homespun look.

TROUSERS

6 Place the four denim trouser pieces into two pairs with right sides together. Pin and backstitch along the curved seam from the waist edge to the crotch on both sets of trouser pieces.

7 Open up the two trouser pieces and place them together with the right sides facing and the crotch seams matching. Backstitch all the way along the two inside leg seams. Similarly, backstitch the two outside leg seams.

8 Turn the trousers to the right side. Pull away loose threads at the waist and trouser bottoms to encourage fraying. Take a tiny square of contrast fabric, turn under the raw edges and hand stitch it to one leg of the trousers to form a patch. Again, also use contrast thread and big stitches to secure the patch.

HAT

9 Pin the two hat brim pieces together with the wrong sides facing and, with a contrasting thread, oversew around the edge. Join together the two short edges of the hat band to form a circle. Press open the seam. Pin the 'circle' inside the brim, right sides facing, and with the brim uppermost, backstitch in place. Turn to the wrong side.

10 Pin the hat top piece to the hat band and, working with the top uppermost, backstitch in place. Turn the hat through to the right side.

BOOTS

11 Pin the four boot pieces together in pairs to make the two individual boots. With brown sewing thread in the needle, oversew around the edges working the stitches close together. Leave the top edge open.

12 Following the diagram and using the lighter embroidery thread, stitch a shoelace pattern on the front of the boots. Leave sufficient thread in each boot to tie in a bow.

Leave open

B

ARM
cut
4

Leave open

Leave open

A

HEAD
AND
BODY

cut 2

Leave open

PATTERN PIECES FOR GIRL DOLL

- Patterns for this project are life size and
- do not need to be enlarged. Before
- pinning on the pattern pieces, see the
- Checklist on page 62.

Cutting layout for calico

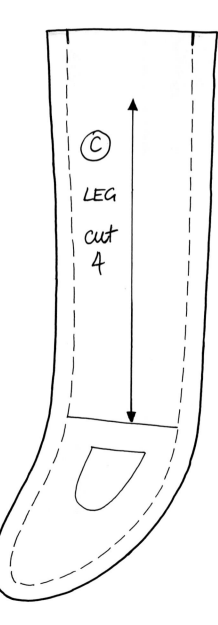

GIRL DOLL ~
HEAD AND BODY

1 Pin the two head and body pieces together right sides inside, and machine stitch around taking a 6mm (¼in) seam. Leave the bottom edge open for turning through and the two openings at each side for the arms. Using small scissors, snip into the curved seam allowance, just short of the stitches, and turn through to the right side.

2 Use the end of a knitting needle to push out any tight corners. Stuff, beginning with the head. Again, you may need to use the end of the knitting needle to help push the stuffing well in to give a smooth, rounded shape. Turn in and pin the openings for the arms and then continue to stuff the body. Finger press the turnings on the bottom opening and put the body to one side.

ARMS AND LEGS

3 With the right sides inside, pin the four arm pieces together to make two arms. Machine stitch around, leaving the opening for turning through, as shown on the pattern. Snip into the curved seam allowance and turn through to the right side.

4 Stuff evenly as before. Insert the arms into the body so that they are pointing downwards (first removing the pins) and, with matching thread, backstitch through all four layers to secure.

5 Stitch the leg pieces together in the same way and stuff evenly. Place them inside the bottom edge of the body with the toes pointing outwards. Pin and backstitch through all four layers, as for the arms.

HAIR

6 Following the diagram and working freehand, lightly draw in the hairline with a pencil. Then, with watered-down brown fabric paint and a brush, fill in the hair. Suggest the texture and direction of the hair with lines of running stitches using a darker brown embroidery thread, as shown.

Designed to look hand-made, the stitching does not have to look perfect on these dolls.

FACE

7 Working freehand, lightly draw in the features with a pencil, as shown in the diagram. Fill in the lips and cheeks with watered-down red fabric paint in two strengths; the palest for the cheeks. Outline the eyes and eyebrows with running stitches using one strand of brown embroidery thread. Work the eyes in satin stitch using two strands of blue.

SHOES

8 Lightly draw the outline as shown in the diagram and work the shoes with two strands of green embroidery thread using long and short filling stitches. Add the two pearl buttons to the side, as shown.

CLOTHING PATTERN PIECES FOR GIRL

Patterns for this project are life size and do not need to be enlarged. For the dress, tape the two pattern pieces together before cutting the fabric. Before pinning on the pattern pieces, see the Checklist on page 62.

Join both dress pieces together before cutting fabric ↑

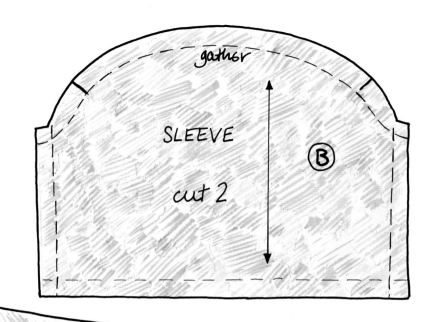

gather

SLEEVE

cut 2

Ⓑ

Ⓒ

PANTALOONS

cut 4

Ⓐ

DRESS

Front and back

cut 2

Other pattern pieces:

For the hat brim Ⓓ, cut 2 circles 10cm (4in) in diameter, with a central hole 2·5cm (1in) in diameter, from the floral fabric.

For the hat top Ⓔ cut 1 circle 5cm (2in) diameter.

For the hat band Ⓕ cut a piece 14cm (5½in) x 3cm (1¼in)

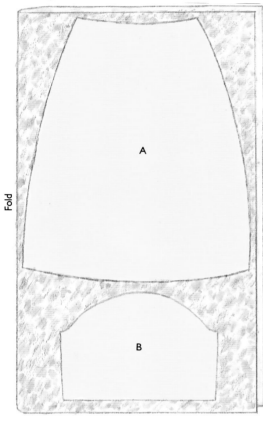

Cutting layout for lawn fabric

Cutting layout for small print cotton fabric

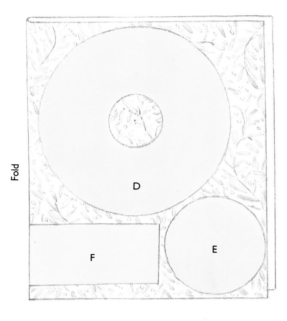

Cutting layout for contrasting printed pattern fabric

GIRL'S CLOTHES ~ DRESS

1 Pin the two dress pieces together with the right sides facing. Either hand sew (backstitch) or machine stitch along each side, leaving the armholes open about 13mm (½in) down from the neck edge, as shown.

2 In the same way, join the underarm seams together on each sleeve, and press the seams open. Run a gathering thread around the sleeve head and pull up the thread until the sleeve fits the armhole. Place the sleeves inside the dress with

the right sides together, aligning the seams and evening the gathers on the sleevehead. Using matching thread, backstitch in place.

3 Decide which is the back of the dress and cut a 4cm (1½in) opening from the neckline down the centre back. Make narrow double turnings on all the raw edges beginning with the back opening, then around the neck, sleeves and the bottom of the dress. Using running stitches and matching sewing thread, pin and stitch to neaten.

4 Turn in the short raw edges of the 13mm (½in) wide lace trim and attach it around the neck edge with neat running stitches. Apply the wider lace trim to the dress hem in the same way and, finally, attach a fabric or lace flower to the centre front neck edge for decoration.

PANTALOONS

5 For each pair of pantaloons, pin the four pantaloon pieces together to make two legs and machine around the curved edge taking a 6mm (¼in) seam. Snip into the seam allowance and press the seams open. Similarly, pin the two sections together and stitch around the inside leg seam in a continuous movement. Stitch the outside leg seams and fingerpress all seams open.

A fabric flower and old lace are pretty touches on the dress.

6 Make narrow double turnings on the waist edge and on the bottom of each leg and secure with tiny running stitches. Apply the lace trim to the inside of each leg and hem stitch it neatly to the turning. Overlap the raw edges of the trim, turn under and secure with one or two stitches.

HAT

7 With the right sides inside, pin the two hat brim pieces together and machine stitch around the outer edge. Trim and clip into the seam allowance and turn through to the right side.

8 Similarly, join together the two short edges of the hat band to form a circle and open the seam. Fit the 'circle' inside the brim, right sides facing, and pin the hat band and the top layer of the brim together. Backstitch in place.

9 Make a narrow turning on the brim lining, clip into the edge if necessary, and slip stitch over the previous seam, to neaten.

10 Pin the hat top to the hat band and, working from the wrong side with the top uppermost, backstitch in place. Turn to the right side finger pressing the seams flat.

11 Apply the lace trim to the underside edge of the brim neatly overlapping the raw edges of the lace and hemming in place. Attach the ribbon by overlapping the ends and stitching on the button to hold. Cut the ribbon tails, as shown, to prevent fraying. To finish, apply one or two fabric flowers to the front of the hat stitching through the ribbon.

TURN YOUR MEMORIES INTO TOYS WITH THESE DELIGHTFUL KEEPSAKE DOLLS.

THEY MAKE THOUGHTFUL GIFTS FOR ADULTS AND OLDER CHILDREN ALIKE AND

ARE AN IDEAL WAY OF MARKING A SPECIAL OCCASION

Designed to look hand-made, these dolls are not at all difficult to make.

To create a genuine memory doll you need some pieces of fabric, scraps of lace or ribbon, bits of jewellery or other tiny objects that have a sentimental appeal for you.

Scraps of fabric from wedding or christening gowns are ideal for memory dolls - as are beads and tiny brooches. Putting a pocket on the doll means you can find a home for a ring, a message or a child's first tooth!

MEMORY DOLLS

MATERIALS

GIRL DOLL (measures 22cm (8½in) high)

BODY

- 15cm × 30cm (6in × 12in) of lightweight white cotton fabric, such as lawn, for the body
- 7cm × 20cm (6in × 8in) of narrow striped lightweight cotton fabric (any colour) for the legs
- Loose polyester filling or kapok
- Cold tea (optional)
- Stranded embroidery thread in red, brown, black and blue for the shoes, hair and face details

BLOUSE AND SKIRT

- 39cm × 24cm (15½in × 9½in) of lightweight cotton fabric with a small printed pattern
- 40cm (16in) of old lace trim, approx 2cm (¾in) wide, for the sleeve edges
- 30cm (12in) of 14mm (½in) wide trim, such as that used for a wedding dress or christening gown, with sentimental value, to trim the skirt hem
- Green and blue embroidery threads
- Three press studs
- Three tiny buttons for the blouse

BONNET AND PANTALOONS

- 33cm × 24cm (13in × 9½in) of lightweight cotton fabric with a contrasting tiny printed pattern
- 35cm (14in) of old lace trim, 13mm (½in) wide

SHAWL

- 36cm × 9cm (14in × 3½in) of old lace with one decorative edge for the shawl

JEWELLERY

- A small brooch or other piece of jewellery (with sentimental value) for attaching to the doll

Body fabric before antiquing

Pantaloon fabric

Striped leg fabric

Fabric for the dress

Trimmings and accessories

MATERIALS

BOY DOLL (measures 22cm (8½in) high)

BODY

- 32cm × 21cm (12in × 8½in) of lightweight cotton fabric, such as lawn, for the body
- Loose polyester filling or kapok
- Cold tea (optional)
- Embroidery threads in black, brown, red and blue

SHIRT

- 17cm × 24cm (7in × 9½in) of miniature checked or striped cotton fabric
- Two small press studs
- Two brown old buttons

TROUSERS AND WAISTCOAT

- 22cm × 25cm (8½in × 10in) of grey flannel or other similar fabric
- Two odd pearl buttons approx 1cm (⅜in) across for the trousers
- Green embroidery thread

Grey flannel and tiny check for the boy's clothes

Embroidery thread

DOLL PATTERN PIECES

- Patterns for this project are life size and do not need to be enlarged. Before pinning on the pattern pieces, see the Checklist on this page.

GIRL HEAD AND BODY

cut 2

(A)

leave open

LEG

(C)

cut 4

leave open

ARM

(D)

cut 4

leave open

BOY HEAD AND BODY

(B)

cut 2

leave open

CHECKLIST

- Trace off the outline of the actual size pattern pieces, transfer all marks and cut out, see pages 6-7.
- Wash and press all new fabrics to test for shrinkage. "Antique" both the doll fabric and the clothes fabric, see page 6.
- Cut out the required number for each pattern piece from the appropriate fabric.
- Set your sewing machine to the correct stitch, length and tension and do a test run on your chosen fabric, see page 8.
- Seam allowances are included (except for the skirt, see step instructions) and should be stitched and trimmed back to 3mm (⅛in), see page 8.

Fold

C

Cutting layout for striped cotton

Cutting layout for lightweight cotton lawn

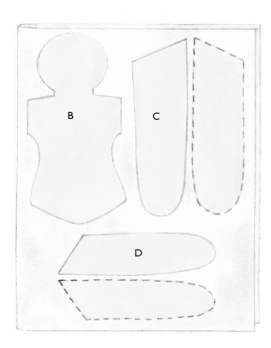

Cutting layout for white cotton

GIRL DOLL ~ HEAD AND BODY

1 Pin and tack the two head and body pieces together with the right sides inside. Machine stitch around taking 6mm (¼in) seams and leaving a 2.5cm (1in) opening at one side of the body as shown on the pattern. Double stitch down each side of the neck for extra strength.

2 With small scissors, carefully snip into the curved seam allowances at the neck and around the head and waist. Trim back the seams to 3mm (⅛in) to reduce bulk around the head and neck.

3 Turn through to the right side using a knitting needle to help push out any awkward corners. If you want to give the doll an 'antique' look simply dip the unstuffed pieces into cold tea and leave to dry before pressing them.

4 Stuff the body and head piece, starting with the head. Remember to tease out the stuffing and aim at a smooth finish and a well shaped body and head. Use the end of a knitting needle to help push the stuffing well into the corners. Turn in the raw edges of the opening and, with matching sewing thread, neatly oversew to close.

ARMS AND LEGS

5 With the right sides inside, pin and tack the arm pieces together to make two arms. Machine stitch around taking a 6mm (¼in) seam and leaving the short straight side open. Machine stitch the legs in the same way. Snip into the curved seams, turn both the arms and legs to the right side and stuff.

Legs in a different fabric add a special touch to this doll.

6 Turn in the raw edges of the openings and, with matching sewing thread, oversew to close. It is important to turn under the edges evenly on both the arms and legs to ensure that they are the same length when finished.

7 Following the diagram for the correct position, attach both the legs and arms to the body using matching sewing thread and small oversewing stitches. Notice that the long side of the arm extends from the neck and forms the top of the arm and that the longer side of the leg extends from the hip and forms the outside of the leg.

HAIR

8 Using two or three strands of brown embroidery thread in your needle, knot the end and stitch evenly all over the back of the head and around the face with small looped stitches. To work the stitch, make two backstitches into the same hole but, instead of pulling the first stitch through, leave a small loop. The loop is secured by the second stitch. Continue to sew loops to cover the entire head.

FACE

9 For the face details, first mark out the eyes, eyebrows, lips and cheeks with a very light pencil line as shown in the pattern. Using the appropriate coloured embroidery threads, with a single strand in your needle, neatly embroider the eyes and cheeks in satin stitch, the lips and eyebrows in stem stitch and outline the eyes and cheeks with backstitch. Take the needle to the back of the head to start and finish inside the hair.

SHOES

Boy shoe   Girl shoe

10 To embroider the shoes, first follow the diagram and lightly pencil in the outline of the shoes onto the feet. Using red embroidery thread, fill in the shoe area with long and short stitch.

BOY DOLL ~ HEAD AND BODY

1 For the boy doll cut out the pattern pieces following the cutting layout and then continue to make up the doll following the instructions for the girl memory doll until you are ready to embroider the face details and shoes.

2 For the boy's hair, use black embroidery thread and stitch looped backstitches to cover the head, as for the girl, see step 8.

3 For the face, embroider in exactly the same way as for the girl doll omitting her red cheeks and adding a black moustache filled in with rows of stem stitching (see the pattern).

4 Using black embroidery thread, embroider the shoes in the same way as for the girl but notice that the boy's shoes have a square buckle in front.

CLOTHING PATTERN PIECES
FOR GIRL

- Patterns for this project are life size and do not need to be enlarged. Pantaloon pattern piece is on page 83. Before pinning on the pattern pieces, see the checklist on page 75.

M DRAWSTRING cut 1

place on fold

B SKIRT WAISTBAND

cut 1

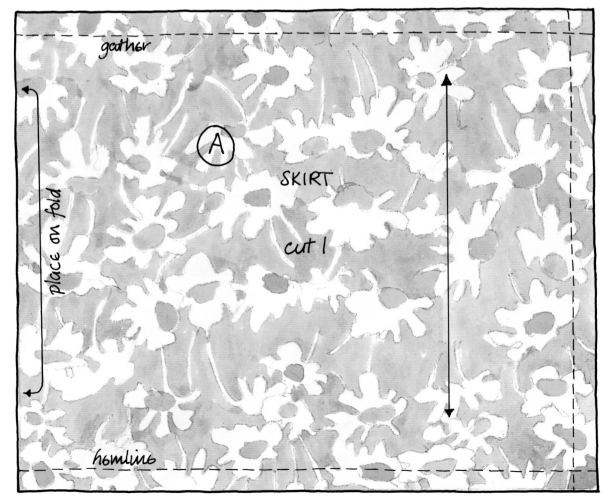

gather

A

SKIRT

cut 1

place on fold

hemline

CB

D

BLOUSE BACK

facing

G

cut 2 BACK FACING

gather

E SLEEVE cut 2

BONNET TIES cut 2 L

C BLOUSE FRONT cut 1

gather

H BONNET cut 1

place on fold

J BONNET FRONT FACING cut 1

F FRONT FACING cut 1

place on fold

K BONNET BOTTOM FRILL cut 1

Cutting layout for small print cotton fabric

Fold

A

C

F

E D B

G

Fold

L

M

K

J H

*Cutting layout for lightweight cotton fabric
with tiny contrasting printed pattern*

GIRL'S CLOTHES ~ PANTALOONS

1 For the pantaloons, use the trouser/pantaloon pattern piece on page 83. Pin the four leg pieces right sides together to make two legs. Tack and machine stitch along the curved edge. Snip into the curved seam just short of the stitching and press the seam open. Repeat on the second leg.

2 With right sides inside, pin, tack and machine stitch the two pieces together, stitching the inner leg seams in one continuous movement. Pin, tack and machine stitch the two outer seams of the pantaloons. Press the seams open.

3 Press to the wrong side an 8mm (5/16in) double turning along the waist edge of the pantaloons and pin. Using matching sewing thread, hem to secure the turning.

4 Turn the pantaloons to the right side and, using small scissors, make an upright slit through single fabric at the front of drawstring channel. Buttonhole stitch around the slit to prevent it from fraying.

5 Make narrow double turnings on each leg of the pantaloons and hem using matching sewing thread. Add the lace trim by hand, pinning to the wrong side of the leg hem and securing with small running stitches through a single layer of fabric. As an optional extra, you could decorate the pantaloon bottoms with a row of embroidery, such as chainstitch, feather stitch, or French knots, in a contrasting colour.

6 To make the drawstring, turn each short end of the fabric under 6mm (¼in) and press. Fold each long side towards the centre so that the two edges meet. Fold over once more and hand stitch to secure, using tiny running stitches. Attach a small safety pin to one end of the drawstring and thread it through the waist channel.

BLOUSE

7 Pin the blouse front and the blouse front facing together, with the right sides inside and the necklines matching. Tack and then machine stitch around the neckline. Repeat on the two blouse back pieces.

8 Using small scissors, snip into the seam allowance just short of the stitch line. Turn the facing to the wrong side and press the neck edge.

9 Pin the front and two back pieces right sides inside. Tack and machine stitch along the shoulder and side seams. Remove all tacking stitches and press the seams open.

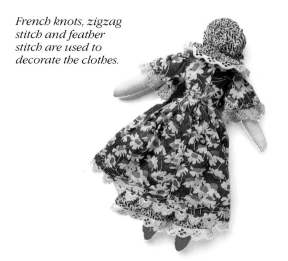

French knots, zigzag stitch and feather stitch are used to decorate the clothes.

10 On each sleeve, pin and tack the two underarm edges together with the right sides inside, then machine stitch using matching sewing thread. Make a line of gathering stitches around the sleeve head. Pull up the gathers so that the sleeve fits the armhole, and secure the thread. Even the gathers.

11 With right sides together, pin, tack and machine stitch the sleeves in place. You may find it easier to hand stitch the sleeves using tiny backstitches and matching thread. Clip into the curved seams.

12 Make a double turning of 6mm (¼in) on both sides of the back opening and neatly slip stitch. Attach two press studs: one at the neck and one about 2.5cm (1in) lower. Make a narrow hem on the bottom edge of the blouse and slip stitch around.

13 Similarly, turn up the edges of the sleeves and apply the lace trim to the wrong side. Cut the lace into two equal lengths and join the two short sides together to form two rings. Either gather or pleat the straight edge and pin to the sleeve. Adjust the gathers or pleats to fit and hand stitch in place with small running stitches. Repeat on the second sleeve.

14 Sew the three buttons to the centre front of the blouse. Using bright embroidery thread, decorate around the sleeves with a row of zigzag stitch and the neck with blanket stitch.

SKIRT

15 Working on the right side of the skirt section, pleat along one long edge making 6mm (¼in) deep pleats close together so that the pleated edge fits the waistband. Pin each pleat and tack within the seam allowance using small stitches.

16 Fold the section right side inside and pin the centre back seam together taking a 1cm (⅜in) allowance. Tack and machine stitch up to the opening, about 2.5cm (1in) from the waist edge. Press the seam open. Make narrow double turnings on both sides of the opening and neatly hem using matching sewing thread.

17 With the right sides inside, pin the waistband to the waist edge of the skirt with the seam allowances extending beyond the opening. Tack and machine stitch in place.

18 Turn over the short edges of the waistband to the wrong side, making 6mm (¼in) turnings, and press. Fold the waistband in half, make a single 6mm (¼in) turning on the long edge and pin it to the wrong side of the waistband. Using matching thread, hem in place catching the previous machine stitching.

To make the shawl, you could use scraps from a christening gown or bridal veil.

19 For the hem, fold over a narrow 4mm (⅛in) turning and then a 6mm (¼in) turning. Pin, tack and slip stitch with matching sewing thread. Working on the wrong side, attach the lace trim to the outer edge of the hem with running stitches neatly overlapping the raw edge to finish.

20 Using bright green embroidery thread, add a border of feather stitching to finish the hem. Decorate the waistband with a row of bright blue French knots spaced 6mm (¼in) apart. Stitch the press stud to the waistband to close the opening.

BONNET

21 Make a line of gathering stitches along the bottom of the bonnet, gently gather and secure the thread. Place the bonnet frill right sides together along the bottom of the bonnet, pleat to fit the gathered edge of the bonnet. Stitch the frill in place. Make a single turning to the wrong side along the bottom and press the frill downwards.

22 Make a line of small gathering stitches along the curved edge of the main bonnet piece. Pull up the gathers to fit the front facing section. Secure the thread firmly.

23 Place the front facing along the gathered edge of the bonnet, with right sides together and the edges aligned. There should be 6mm (¼in) left over at each end to turn under. Hand stitch using small running stitches. Turn the front facing to the wrong side of the bonnet. Make a narrow turning and neatly slip stitch to hold.

24 Using tiny running stitches, attach lace trim along the bottom edge of the frill turning in the two raw edges of trim to neaten. To make the ties, simply fold over the two long edges so that they meet in the middle. Fold over once more and hand stitch, turning under each end and securing with one or two stitches. Attach one tie to each side of the bonnet, with small stitches. Add a line of embroidery stitches to the front band of the bonnet, using French knots, zigzag stitch, or chain stitch as preferred.

SHAWL AND JEWELLERY

25 The ideal lace edging will have deep decorative scallops or points and a fine mesh ground. Simply hem a narrow turning on each short edge and a similar turning on the neck edge. Gather this edge to fit around your doll and secure the thread. Attach a favourite brooch to fasten at the neck or a length of pearl necklace, as shown here.

CLOTHING PATTERN PIECES
FOR BOY

- Patterns for this project are life size and
- do not need to be enlarged. Before
- pinning on the pattern pieces, turn to the
- Checklist on page 75.

A

SHIRT
BACK

cut 1

gather

C

SLEEVE

cut 2

D

BACK FACING
cut 1

FRONT
FACING
cut 2

E

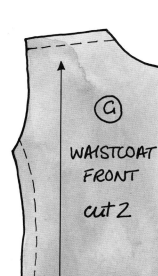

H

TROUSERS
AND
PANTALOONS

cut 4

G

WAISTCOAT
FRONT

cut 2

F

WAISTCOAT
BACK

cut 1

B

SHIRT
FRONT

cut 2

J
POCKET
cut 1

K   BRACES   cut 2

Cutting layout for miniature checked fabric

Cutting layout for grey flannel

BOY'S CLOTHES ~ SHIRT

1 With the right sides inside, place the back facing onto the shirt back section with the edges of the neck and shoulders matching. Hand stitch around the neckline with small running stitches. Do the same on both shirt fronts.

2 Snip into the curved seam allowance just short of the stitching, and turn the facings to the wrong side. Press the neck edge. Place the two shirt fronts onto the shirt back with the right sides together. Lift up the facings and handsew along the facing, shoulder seams and side seams.

3 Join together the underarm seams on both sleeves using running stitches. Finger press the seams open. Insert the sleeves into the armhole with the right sides inside aligning the underarm sleeve with the side seam of the shirt. Ease with tiny gathers or pleats, if necessary and, using tiny running stitches, hand sew in place.

4 Turn under and stitch with small running stitches the bottom edge of the shirt, then do the same for the two front seams and the sleeves.

For the hair, black embroidery thread is sewn in loops.

5 Attach two press studs to the front of the shirt about 2.5cm (1in) apart and then sew the two buttons on top.

TROUSERS

6 With the right sides inside, join the four trouser leg pieces together to make two legs. Pin and hand stitch around the curved seam using small running stitches. Clip into the curved seam and finger press the seam open.

Bright green embroidery thread is used to work blanket stitch around the jacket edges.

7 Place the two leg sections together right sides inside. Hand stitch the inside leg seams in one continuous operation. Stitch the two side seams and press the seams open.

8 Neaten the waist edge and trouser legs by making a single 6mm (¼in) turning and hand stitching into place using bright green embroidery thread and running stitches.

9 To make the braces, fold the two lengths over and using bright green embroidery thread, stitch down the middle of each one. Attach the braces to the inside waist edge of the trousers at the front and back, with a cross over at the back. Use one or two small stitches to secure.

10 Sew the two pearl buttons to the right side of the trousers where the braces are stitched. Stitch across the top edge of the pocket and pin in place. Turn under these remaining sides and stitch. You can keep something of sentimental value in the memory doll's pocket, for example, your baby's first tooth.

WAISTCOAT

11 Place the two front pieces onto the back piece with the shoulder and side seams matching, and with the right sides inside. Using matching sewing thread, hand stitch to secure. Finger press the seams open.

12 Using bright green embroidery thread, work blanket stitch around the outside edges and both armholes to neaten and decorate the waistcoat. Due to the density of flannel, the edges, as in this case, can be decorated as a single layer without making turnings.

PYJAMA-CASE DOLL

ALL CHILDREN WILL LOVE AN ANGEL WHO WATCHES OVER THEM WHILE THEY SLEEP AND SITS ON THEIR PILLOW, GUARDING THEIR PYJAMAS DURING THE DAY!

Folk art fabrics have been used to make this delightful angel. Whatever materials you choose, the pyjama-case doll is sure to become a treasured toy, kept safely tucked up in a child's bed.

The bottom of the angel's skirt can be opened and closed so nightclothes can be stored inside. If you are making her as a gift for a young child, who may want to cuddle the doll, choose soft, woolly hair. For an older girl or teenager the raffia hair makes an unusual and fun mascot – especially with a little heart popped in her pinafore pocket.

Fabric for the wings and little heart

Cream coloured cotton jersey for the body

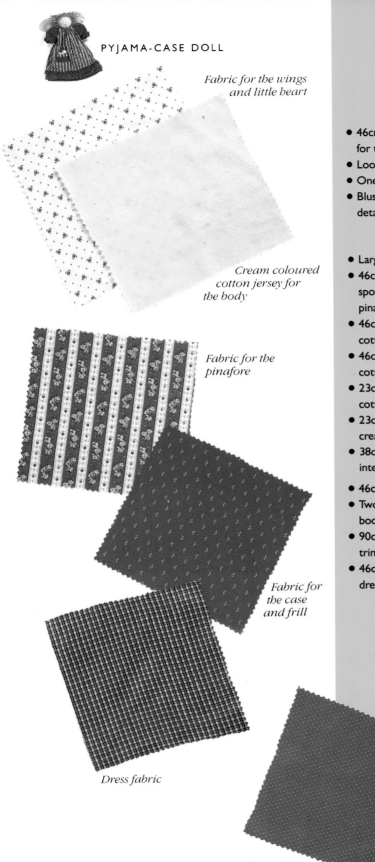

Fabric for the pinafore

Fabric for the case and frill

Dress fabric

Sleeve fabric

MATERIALS

DOLL (measures 50cm (20in) high)
- 46cm (18in) of 112cm (44in) wide cotton jersey for the body
- Loose polyester filling or kapok
- One skein of raffia for the hair
- Blusher and black felt-tipped pen for the face details

CLOTHES AND CASE
- Large chenille needle
- 46cm (18in) of 112cm (44in) wide of large white spot cotton for the case, outside pocket and pinafore frill
- 46cm (18in) of 112cm (44in) wide of red stripe cotton for the pinafore and inside pocket
- 46cm (18in) of 112cm (44in) wide of tiny check cotton for the dress
- 23cm (9in) of 112cm (44in) wide of polka-dot cotton for the sleeves
- 23cm (9in) of 112cm (44in) wide red-spotted cream cotton for the wings and heart
- 38cm × 25cm (15in × 10in) of heavyweight interfacing for the wings
- 46cm (18in) of velcro fastening for the case
- Two large press studs to secure the wings to the body
- 90cm (1yd) of toning 1cm (⅜in) wide ribbon to trim the wings and heart
- 46cm (18in) of 2mm (⅛in) wide ribbon for the dress neck

Ribbon trims and raffia – don't use raffia if you are making this doll for a young child; use yarn instead.

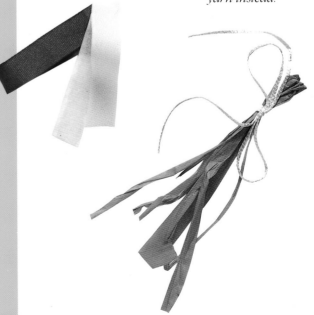

PATTERN PIECES FOR
BODY AND CASE

Patterns for this project should be enlarged to twice the size. If you have access to a photocopier with an enlarging facility set it to 200%. Otherwise trace off the patterns on to a grid, following the procedure outlined on page 7. (See also the Checklist on this page).

A

HEAD
AND
BODY   cut 2

waistline

leave open

B

leave open

ARM

cut 4

Other pattern pieces:
For the pyjama case, C cut one piece 35cm x 90cm (14in x 36in) on the straight grain from the large white spot fabric.

CHECKLIST

- Enlarge the pattern pieces. Transfer all marks and cut out, see pages 6-7.
- Wash and press the main fabrics, see page 6.
- Cut out the required number for each pattern piece from the appropriate fabric, see page 7. For the dress skirt, pinafore frill and pocket, see the box opposite.
- Set your sewing machine to the correct stitch, length and tension and do a test run on your chosen fabric, see page 8.
- Seam allowances are included throughout. Unless otherwise stated, stitch and trim back to 6mm (¼in), snip into curved seams and press open, see page 8.

C

F

E

Cutting layout for red/white spot fabric

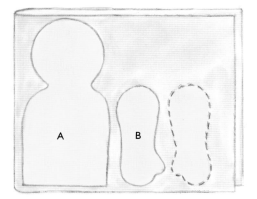

A

B

Cutting layout for cotton jersey

PYJAMA-CASE DOLL

*Back view
of the wings*

ARMS

2 Pin the four arm pieces together, with right sides facing, in pairs. Machine stitch around leaving an opening as shown. Trim and clip the seams before turning through to the right side. Insert the filling, turn in the raw edges of the opening and oversew to close. Using the chenille needle, sew the arms to the body by hand at the points marked on the pattern.

THE BODY AND CASE ~
BODY

1 With the right sides facing, machine stitch the two body pieces together on the stitching line leaving the bottom edge open as shown. Trim and clip the seams where necessary and turn through to the right side. Turn in and tack the seam allowance of the opening. Insert the filling using a knitting needle to push it evenly into the head and body. Oversew the opening to close.

FACE AND HAIR

3 Using a fine black felt-tipped pen, mark the eyes as shown on the pattern. Suggest the cheeks by brushing the face lightly with blusher. To make the hair, cut the raffia into uneven lengths of about 13cm (5in) and, with the chenille needle, thread each length separately through the fabric, working around the face and over the back of the head. Knot the ends firmly together to hold each length in place and space the strands evenly to cover the head. The mouth can be embroidered or drawn on.

CASE

4 With right sides facing, machine stitch the two short sides together to make the side seam of the case. Press the seam open. Turn up and tack a 2.5cm (1in) hem along one long edge. Cut the velcro to measure about 2.5cm (1in) less than half the width of the case. Machine stitch one of the strips to the back and one to the front of the hem edge, stitching along both sides of the tape. About 8cm (3in) from the waist edge, stitch a line across the top of the case (through both layers) to form a pocket for the body of the doll.

5 Using a long machine stitch, make a row of gathering stitches along the waist edge of the case. Pull up the gathers until they fit around the waist of the doll and then backstitch the case to the doll along the waistline, as marked.

PATTERN PIECES FOR DRESS
AND WINGS

Patterns for this project should be enlarged to twice the size. If you have access to a photocopier with an enlarging facility set it to 200%. Otherwise trace off the patterns on to a grid, following the procedure outlined on page 7. Pattern Pieces are continued overleaf. (See also the Checklist on page 89).

Other pattern pieces:
From the large spot fabric, cut the following rectangles on the straight grain:
Pinafore frill Ⓕ, 2 pieces 7.5cm x 90cm (3in x 36in)
Outside pocket Ⓔ, 11.5 cm (4½ in) squares
From the red striped fabric, cut the inside pocket Ⓔ 11.5cm (4½in) square

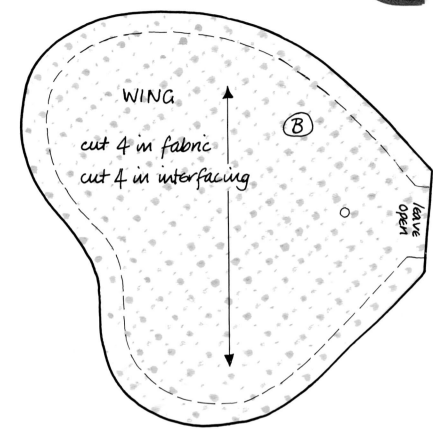

WING

cut 4 in fabric
cut 4 in interfacing

Ⓑ

leave open

Ⓐ

PINAFORE

cut 2

place on fold

neckline

armhole

armhole

BODICE
cut 2

C

Other pattern pieces:

For the dress skirt G cut one rectangle on the straight grain 35.5cm x 90cm (4in x 36in) from the tiny check cotton.

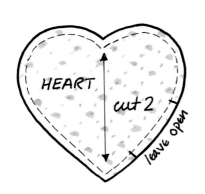

HEART
cut 2

leave open

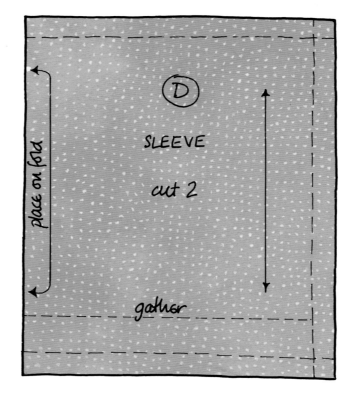

place on fold

SLEEVE

cut 2

D

gather

C

G

Cutting layout for tiny check fabric

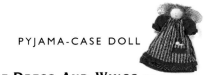

THE DRESS AND WINGS ~
DRESS

Cutting layout for white/red spot fabric

Cutting layout for red and cream stripe
Pocket cut from single layer only

Cutting layout for polka-dot fabric

1 Machine stitch the shoulder seams of the bodice together, with the right sides facing, and leaving the neckline open. Press the shoulder seams open and the seam allowance of the neck to the inside.

2 Using a long machine stitch, make a row of gathering stitches along the top edge of the sleeve. Turn in and machine stitch a 6mm (¼in) hem along the lower wrist edge. Make a second row of gathering stitches 2cm (¾in) in from the hem.

3 Pull up the gathers on the sleeve head until it is the same length as the armhole between the notches. Then, with the right sides facing, stitch the sleeve to the bodice armhole. Similarly, stitch the side seams of the bodice and the underarm seam of the sleeve in a continuous movement.

4 Working on the wrong side, stitch the short sides of the skirt piece together and press the seam open. Make a row of gathering stitches along one raw edge of the skirt, just inside the seam allowance, and a 13mm (½in) hem along the other. Pull up the gathers until the skirt fits the bodice waistline. With the right sides facing, machine stitch the skirt to the bodice.

5 Put the dress on the doll and, using a fairly long running stitch, sew narrow ribbon around the neck about 6mm (¼in) from the edge. Pull up the stitches until the neck fits the doll and tie with a bow in the centre front. Pull up the gathers at the wrist edge of the sleeves and fasten off securely.

6 Make a row of gathering stitches along the neckline of the back and front pinafore pieces. Pull up the gathers on each piece to a length of 5.5cm (2¼in). With the right sides facing, stitch the shoulder seams together and open the seam. Carefully clip into the corners of the neckline, make a narrow single turning all round and machine stitch in place.

This homespun angel could also be made up in fabrics to match your bed linen.

7 With the right sides facing, stitch the side seams together and press them open. Neaten the armholes with a single turning and machine stitch around.

94

MAKING THE WINGS

8 Working on the wrong side, stitch the two frill pieces together along both short sides. Turn to the right side, fold the strip in half lengthways and make a row of gathering stitches through both layers just inside the seamline. Draw up the gathers until the frill is the same size as the hem of the pinafore. With both right sides facing, stitch the frill to the hem and then press the seam allowances upwards.

The keepsake heart fits snugly into the doll's pocket.

11 Using herringbone stitch, attach one piece of interfacing to the wrong side of each of two wing pieces and then, with right sides inside, pin the four wing pieces together to make one pair of wings. Machine stitch around leaving an opening as marked on the pattern. Turn to the right side, press and join the two wings together by machine stitching along the centre seam. Tie the ribbon tightly around the seam to cover the join.

KEEPSAKE HEART

9 With the right sides facing, stitch the two pocket pieces together leaving a 4cm (1½in) opening on one side for turning through after sewing. Press and slip stitch the opening closed. With the wrong side of the pocket to the right side of the pinafore, pin the pocket in place as shown on the pattern. Stitch around to within 2.5cm (1in) of the top edge so that the pocket flap can be folded over to the right side.

10 With right sides inside, stitch the two heart pieces together taking a 6mm (¼in) seam and leaving an opening for turning through to the right side. Stuff evenly and oversew the opening to close. Using tiny hemming stitches, attach a 10cm (4in) length of ribbon to the centre top of the heart to form a loop. The heart can then easily be removed from the pocket or hung around the doll's wrist.

12 To secure the wings, sew a half press stud to the underside of each wing and the matching half to the back shoulder strap of the pinafore on each side, as shown on the pattern.

DUNGAREES, PANTALOONS AND

PETTICOATS — THE COUNTRY

COUSINS HAVE PUT ON THEIR

SMARTEST CLOTHES AND WILL

MAKE A TALKING-POINT SITTING

IN YOUR COUNTRY-STYLE KITCHEN

COUNTRY COUSINS

Separate pattern pieces for the arms and legs and clever finger detailing ensure the country cousins are very attractive dolls while still being easy to make.

The clothes are simple but smart: the boy has his new pair of dungarees on, with a bow-tie and matching handkerchief to smarten it up for Sunday best; the little girl has a floral print dress and matching lacy pantaloons and petticoat.

Choose your own colours for the hair and clothes, perhaps to match the decor in one of your rooms, as you are bound to want to display this charming pair.

MATERIALS

DOLLS (measure 50cm (20in) high)

- 90cm (1yd) of 112cm (44in) wide calico for the two bodices
- Polyester filling or kapok
- 60g (2oz) of chunky knitting wool for the girl's hair
- 60g (2oz) of double knitting wool for the boy's hair
- 46cm (18in) of 13mm (½in) wide tape to match the hair colour of your choice
- Four safety plastic eyes
- 90cm (1yd) of 2cm (¾in) wide ribbon in a contrasting colour for girl doll's hair
- Black and red fine felt-tipped pens and pink blusher for the face details
- Fabric adhesive

BOY'S TROUSERS

- 46cm (18in) of 90cm (36in) wide denim fabric
- Two mini poppa studs

BOY'S SHIRT

- 46cm (18in) of 90cm (36in) wide narrow-striped cotton fabric
- 18cm (7in) of 13mm (½in) wide bias binding to match
- Four small buttons approx 1cm (⅜in) across
- 46cm (18in) of 13mm (½in) wide elastic
- Three press studs 1cm (⅜in) across

BOW TIE AND HANKIE

- 18cm (8in) square of floral print cotton fabric
- 23cm (9in) length of round elastic
- 13cm (5in) square of fabric to match the bow tie

BOY'S BOOTS

- 25cm (10in) square of soft leather
- 1.8m (2yds) of thick crochet cotton for the laces

Calico

Fabrics for boy's clothes

Knitting wool for hair

Fabrics for girl's clothes

Felt and leather

Safety eyes, buttons and braid for laces.

GIRL'S UNDERSKIRT AND PANTALOONS

- 30cm (12in) of 152cm (60in) wide white cotton broderie anglaise
- 50cm (20in) of 4mm (⅛in) wide elastic
- 1.8m (2yds) of white broderie anglaise trim, 3cm (1¼in) wide

GIRL'S DRESS

- 46cm (18in) of 90cm (36in) wide cotton with small floral print
- Four small buttons, approx 1cm (⅜in) across
- Three press studs, 6mm (¼in) across
- Shirring elastic

GIRL'S BOOTS

- 20cm (8in) square of felt
- 90cm (1yd) of thin braid for the laces

DOLL PATTERN PIECES

- Patterns for this project should be
  enlarged to twice the size. If you have
  access to a photocopier with an enlarging
  facility set it to 200%. Otherwise trace off
  the patterns on to a grid, following the
  procedure outlined on page 7.
  (See also the Checklist on this page)

HEAD
AND
BODY

Ⓐ

cut 2

leave open

leave open

Ⓑ

LEG

cut 4

leave open

ARM   cut 4

Ⓒ

CHECKLIST

- Enlarge the pattern pieces. Transfer all marks and
  cut out, see pages 6-7.
- Wash and press the main fabrics, see page 6.
- Cut out the required number for each pattern
  piece from the appropriate fabric, see page 7.
- Set your sewing machine to the correct stitch,
  length and tension and do a test run on your
  chosen fabric, see page 8.
- Seam allowances are included throughout.
  Unless otherwise stated, stitch and trim back
  to 6mm (¼in), snip into curved seams
  and press open, see page 8.

Fold

B   C   A

Cutting layout for calico

THE DOLL ~ BODY AND HEAD

1 Pin, tack and machine stitch the two head and body pieces together with the right sides facing and leaving the lower edge open where indicated on the pattern. Turn over the seam allowance of the opening and press with your fingers.

2 Turn to the right side and insert the plastic eyes into the fabric in the positions shown, securing them firmly at the back with the manufacturer's safety locking device supplied. Stuff the head and body evenly using a large knitting needle to help push the filling in place.

LEGS

3 Pin, tack and machine stitch the leg pieces with the right sides together to form two pairs, leaving the top edge open as indicated on the pattern. Turn the legs through to the right side and stuff to within 2.5cm (1in) of the top.

4 Bring the two seams together at the centre of the leg and make an inverted pleat at each side so that the legs will fit easily into the base of the body. Pin the legs in position and then tack and machine stitch across.

ARMS

5 Pin, tack and machine stitch the four arm pieces together to form two pairs, leaving the top edge open as shown on the pattern. Turn over the seam allowance of the opening and finger press.

6 Turn the arms through to the right side and stuff to within 2.5cm (1in) of the top. Make an inverted pleat at the top of the arm as shown and then oversew the edges together by hand. Pin the arms to the body as shown on the pattern and oversew by hand.

7 Define the fingers by back stitching along the finger lines as shown on the pattern. Complete the face by drawing in two tiny nostrils using black felt pen, the mouth in red pen, and suggest the cheeks with a light dusting of pink blusher.

BOY'S HAIR

8 Cut sufficient 25cm (10in) lengths of wool to cover the head thickly. Lay the wool in parallel strands across the 13cm (5in) length of tape leaving 13mm (½in) turnings at each end. Machine stitch the wool to the tape.

9 Cut several 13cm (5in) lengths of wool for the fringe and stick these first to the centre of the head with the ends hanging unevenly over the forehead.

10 Apply glue to the tape and then cover the stuck ends of the fringe with the tape allowing it to run from the top of the head to the neckline. Trim the wool to the required length and glue it to the neckline and to the hairline around the face.

Hair: front and back view.

GIRL'S HAIR

11 For the fringe cut about 20 lengths of wool 15cm (6in) long. Using a length of yarn, tie them together in the centre and glue into position in the middle of the head. Trim the ends to uneven lengths and unravel some of the yarn to give a curled effect.

12 Cut about 80 lengths of wool 66cm (26in) long and tie them together in the centre. Machine stitch the wool on to a 13cm (5in) length of tape using a long machine stitch. Place the tape along the centre back of the head behind the fringe and glue into place.

13 Bring the strands forward and glue in place along the hairline around the face and neck. Cut some of the strands near the face short and plait the remaining lengths. Secure each plait with a ribbon bow and stitch it in place.

14 Cut 40 lengths of wool 20cm (8in) long and tie them together in the centre. Glue the centre of the hank to the top of the head behind the fringe and then trim and unravel as before.

CLOTHING PATTERN PIECES
FOR BOY

- Patterns for this project should be enlarged to twice the size. If you have access to a photocopier with an enlarging facility set it to 200%. Otherwise trace off the patterns on to a grid, following the procedure outlined on page 7.
- (See also the Checklist on page 99).

CB
strap
leave open

(A)

TROUSER
BACK

cut 2

pleat

leave open

CF

B

TROUSER
FRONT

cut 2

gather

G

SLEEVE

cut 2

hemline

J

COLLAR

cut 2

C

BIB FRONT
cut 2

K

BOOT

cut 4

E

BACK
POCKET
cut 1

D

FRONT
POCKET

cut 1

H

SHIRT FRONT
cut 2

SHIRT BACK
cut 1 with CB
dotted line
on a fold

CF
CB

L

BOOT
SOLE

cut 2

F   TROUSER STRAP   cut 2

leave open

Cutting layout for narrow-striped fabric

Cutting layout for denim fabric

The bow tie and pocket handkerchief match the girl doll's dress.

THE BOY'S CLOTHES ~ SHIRT

1 Pin, tack and machine stitch the back and front shoulder seams together with the right sides inside. Press the seams open. With the right sides facing, stitch the collar pieces together around the outer curved edge only. Trim, snip into the curved seam and turn through to the right side. Press and topstitch 2mm (⅛in) from the finished edge.

2 Pin and tack the wrong side of the collar to the right side of the shirt neckline between the centre front notches. Tack the bias binding on top of the collar, matching the seamlines and then machine stitch through all thicknesses. Turn the binding over the raw edge of the neckline and hem stitch to the machine stitching on the wrong side.

3 On each shirt front, turn the facing to the right side along the foldline and stitch across the remaining neckline. Turn through to the wrong side and press the foldlines.

4 Gather the sleeve head between the notches as shown in the diagram and also along the wrist edge using a long machine stitch. Pull up the gathering stitches on the sleeve head so that it is the same length as the shirt armhole. With the right sides together, pin, tack and machine stitch the sleeve in place, neatly evening out the gathers as necessary to fit.

5 With the right sides together and the seams matching, join the underarm seam and the shirt side seam in one continuous operation. Press the seam open.

6 Turn up a 2.5cm (1in) hem at the wrist edge of each sleeve and machine stitch in place. Stitch a second row close to the folded edge. Thread sufficient elastic through each hem to make the sleeve fit at the doll's wrist. Overlap the elastic at each end and hem stitch together to hold.

7 Make a narrow hem along the lower edge of the shirt and machine stitch across. Sew on the buttons where indicated on the pattern and then sew the two press studs, where required, to fasten the centre front.

TROUSERS

8 To make the two pockets, turn under the seam allowances on the side and lower edges and machine stitch 6mm (¼in) in from the edge. Turn under the top edge and stitch 13mm (½in) in from the edge. Machine stitch the appropriate pocket to the front right leg and back left leg pieces as shown on the pattern, placing the wrong side of the pocket to the right side of the trousers and stitching close to the edge.

9 With the right sides facing stitch the two trouser back and front pieces together at the centre front. Snip into the curved seam and press it open. Pin and tack the pleats in place at the waistline of the trouser front pieces.

10 Pin the trouser back and front pieces together with the right sides facing, and stitch the side seams up to the notch as marked on the pattern. Press the seams open. Make single turnings at the side seam openings and along the back waistline. Neaten the raw edges and tack in place.

11 With the right sides facing stitch the outer bib section to the trouser front at the waistline. Press the seams upwards. With right sides facing, stitch the two bib sections together around the outer edges. Snip across the corners, turn through to the right side and press. On the inside bib, turn in the remaining raw edge and hem stitch in place at the waistline.

12 To make the straps, fold each one lengthways in half with the right sides together and machine stitch around leaving one short edge open. Turn through to the right side and top stitch close to the finished edges. Tack the straps in position at the back waistline, as indicated on the pattern, and then stitch all the finished edges, making two rows of stitching at the back waistline to hold the straps firmly in place.

13 Turn up the trouser bottoms to the required length and topstitch in place with two rows of machine stitching. Fix the two poppa studs to the bib front and the straps following the manufacturer's instructions.

BOOTS

14 With the right sides outside, place the four boot sections together in pairs to make two boots. Pin, tack and machine stitch along the back seam and the front seam from the base of the foot to the notch as shown. Working on the wrong side, spread a fine line of glue along the edge of the base of the shoe and the sole. Bring the edges together and press firmly between the fingers until they are firmly attached. Thread the lace through holes in each boot using a strong needle and about 90cm (1yd) of lace for each boot.

BOY'S BOW TIE AND HANKIE

15 Cut two rectangles of fabric, one measuring 7.5cm × 15cm (3in x 6in) and the other 5cm × 3cm (2in × 1¼in). Fold the larger one lengthways in half with the right sides facing and machine stitch together 6mm (¼in) from the raw edge, leaving one short side open. Turn through to the right side and press. Fold the short ends under to meet in the centre and oversew the edges together.

16 In the same way, fold, stitch and turn through the smaller rectangle of fabric. Wrap this around the centre of the bow and oversew the ends together. Thread the elastic through the loop at the back of the bow and tie it around the doll's neck underneath the collar.

17 To make the hankie, machine stitch a narrow hem at all sides of the fabric square.

CLOTHING PATTERN PIECES
FOR GIRL

- Patterns for this project should be enlarged to twice the size. If you have access to a photocopier with an enlarging facility set it to 200%. Otherwise trace off the patterns on to a grid, following the procedure outlined on page 7.
- (See also the Checklist on page 99).

(A) BODICE BACK cut 2

BODICE FRONT cut 1 with CF dotted line on a fold

lining

CF
CB

Other pattern pieces:
For both the underskirt and the dress skirt, cut a rectangle on the straight grain from each fabric:
Underskirt (G), 28cm × 90cm (11in × 36in)
Dress skirt (H), 25cm × 90cm (10in × 36in)
Dress frill (J), 4.5cm × 46cm (1¾in × 18in)

gather

(B) SLEEVE cut 2

guide line for elastic

(C) NECKBAND cut 2

E
BOOT
cut 4

F
BOOT SOLE
cut 2

elastic casing

D

place on fold

PANTALOONS

cut 2

hem/trim line

Fold

D

H

Fold

Cutting layout for broderie anglaise

Fold

H

J

C

B

A

Cutting layout for small floral print

1 Turn up the hem at the ankle, as indicated on the pattern, and tack in place. Pin and tack the trim to the wrong side of the hem and machine stitch across. With the right sides together, pin, tack and machine stitch the inner leg seams of each piece to form a pair. Place one leg inside the other with right sides together then pin, tack and stitch around the centre curved seam.

2 Turn under the seam allowance along the waist edge and stitch in place to form a casing for the elastic. Stitch a second row at the outside edge. On the wrong side, unpick one or two stitches in the first seam and thread about 26cm (10in) of elastic through the casing. Adjust the length for the correct fit, overlap the ends and oversew to secure.

UNDERSKIRT

3 Fold the skirt fabric widthways in half, pin, tack and stitch the centre back seam. Press open. Turn up a 13mm (½in) hem and tack in place. Tack the trim to the inside of the hem and then machine through all thicknesses to secure, overlapping the join at the back seam.

6 Pin and tack the frill to the outer neckband with the right sides together. Place the inner neckband on top of the frill also with right sides together and stitch along the seamline leaving the neck edge open. Turn the neckband to the right side and then pin and tack the outer neckband to the neckline of the bodice and stitch in place. Turn under the seam allowance of the inner neckband and hem stitch on the wrong side.

4 Make a 13mm (½in) hem at the waist edge to form a casing, as for the pantaloons. Thread about 26cm (10in) of elastic through the casing and adjust to fit. Cut two 20cm (8in) lengths of trim for shoulder straps and pin in position at the waist 8cm (3in) either side of the centre front and back. Adjust the length of the straps as required and machine stitch across.

8 Make a row of gathering stitches along the skirt waistline. With right sides facing, stitch the centre back seam to within 6cm (2½in) of the waistline. Press the seam allowance to the wrong side of the opening. Pull up the gathering stitches so that the skirt fits the bodice waistline. With right sides facing, pin, tack and machine stitch the skirt and bodice together. Turn under the facing and slipstitch to the inside of the waist seam.

9 Turn up a small hem on the skirt and machine stitch in place. Sew the four buttons to the centre back lefthand side bodice, and attach the three press studs to secure the opening.

DRESS

5 With the right sides facing, machine stitch the back and front shoulder seams together. Press the seams open. Fold the centre back facings to the wrong side and tack in place. Fold the neck frill with right sides together, pin, tack and stitch both short ends and then turn through to the right side. Make a row of machine gathering stitches on the neck seamline of the frill and pull up the gathers until the frill fits the neckband between the notches.

7 Gather the sleeve head between the notches so that the sleeve fits the armhole. Tack in place, even out the gathers and stitch around. Using shirring elastic in your machine, stitch around the guide line at the wrist and then finish the sleeve with a narrow hem. With right sides facing, pin, tack and machine stitch the underarm and bodice side seams together in a continuous operation.

BOOTS

10 With the right sides facing, place the four boot sections together in pairs to make two boots. Pin, tack and machine stitch along the centre front seam and the back seam below the notch. In the same way, stitch the sole to the base of the boot with the right sides together and then turn it right side out. Thread a 40cm (16in) length of braid through holes as indicated on the pattern. Pierce the holes with a leather punch or a large sewing needle. Tie a bow to finish.

CLASSIC CLOTH DOLL

For more experienced needleworkers, this beautiful doll presents an irresistible challenge. From her rosebud-patterned body to her lacy petticoats, beribboned dress and embroidered face, this doll is perfect in every detail.

It is worth taking time and care over choosing and buying fabrics – remember this doll is a masterpiece in the making and will be treasured for many years!

As with all the dolls, you don't have to copy the fabrics used in our example. Try mixing and matching different swatches of fabric and wool .

Pretty patterned fabric for the body

MATERIALS

DOLL (measures 60cm (24in) high)

- 26cm (10in) of 90cm (36in) wide plain cotton fabric such as calico for body
- 26cm (10in) of 90cm (36in) wide patterned fabric for the body
- 90cm (1yd) of 13mm (½in) wide lace for trimming the seams
- 150g (4oz) ball of black double knitting wool for the hair
- 50cm (20in) of 2.5cm (1in) wide red satin ribbon for hair bow
- Black, blue and red stranded embroidery cotton for facial features
- Loose polyester filling or kapok

UNDERSKIRT AND PANTALOONS

- 90cm (1yd) of 90cm (36in) wide white lawn
- 90cm (1yd) of 13mm (½in) wide white satin ribbon for the belt
- 1.8m (2yd) of 6cm (2½in) wide white lace edging for the hem of the underskirt
- 90cm (1yd) of 2.5cm (1in) wide white broderie anglaise for the hem of the pantaloons
- 90cm (1yd) of 2.5cm (½in) wide white lace for the bodice
- 17cm (6in) of white elastic 6mm (¼in) wide
- Three small press studs

DRESS

- 70cm (27in) of 112cm (44in) wide navy and white spotted cotton fabric for the dress
- 26cm (10in) of white poplin for the collar and cuffs
- 40cm (16in) of 13mm (½in) wide lace edging for the collar
- Three small press studs
- 2m (2¼yd) of 13mm (½in) wide white satin ribbon for the trim
- 90cm (1yd) of 2cm (¾in) wide navy satin ribbon for the belt
- Bias binding to match dress fabric

SHOES

- 20cm (8in) square of red felt
- 50cm (20in) of narrow red cord to tie

STOCKINGS

- A pair of child's socks, smallest size, (striped or plain)

Broderie anglaise and trimming

Navy spotted dress fabric and broderie anglaise

DOLL PATTERN PIECES

Patterns for this project should be enlarged to twice the size. If you have access to a photocopier with an enlarging facility set it to 200%. Otherwise trace off the patterns on to a grid, following the procedure outlined on page 7. (See also the Checklist overleaf).

HEAD   cut 2

(A)

leave open

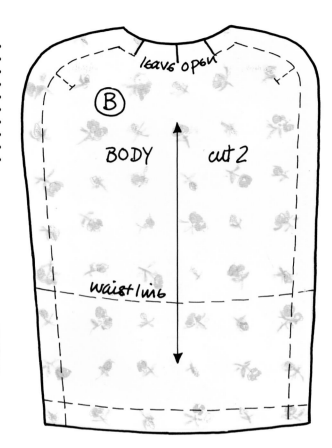

(B)

BODY   cut 2

waistline

leave open

leave open

UPPER LEG

(E)

cut 4

(G)   SOLE

cut 2

leave open

UPPER ARM

(C)

cut 4

(D)

LOWER ARM

cut 4

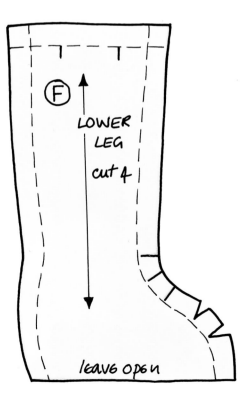

(F)

LOWER LEG

cut 4

leave open

CHECKLIST
....

- Enlarge the pattern pieces. Transfer all marks and cut out, see pages 6-7.
- Wash and press the main fabrics, see page 6.
- Cut out the required number for each pattern piece from the appropriate fabric, see page 7.
- Set your sewing machine to the correct stitch, length and tension and do a test run on your chosen fabric, see page 8.
- Seam allowances are included throughout. Unless otherwise stated, stitch and trim back to 6mm (¼in), snip into the curved seams and press open, see page 8.

Fold

Cutting layout for tiny patterned fabric

2 Using dressmakers' carbon paper, transfer the position and shape of the facial features lightly to the right side of one head piece.

3 Pin, tack and machine stitch the neck darts of both head pieces and then join them together leaving the neck edge open. Turn to the right side and stuff evenly, as before.

THE DOLL ~
BODY AND HEAD
....

1 With the right sides inside, and using machine stitching, join the back and front body pieces together leaving the neck edges open between the notches. Turn over the seam allowance at the neck and fingerpress. Turn right side out and, with the help of a knitting needle, stuff evenly.

Fold

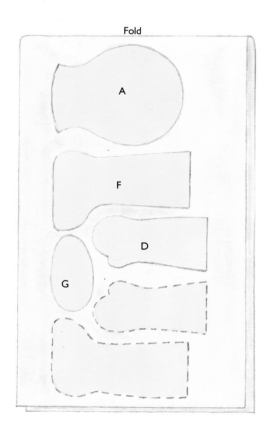

Cutting layout for calico fabric

The classic cloth doll showing the hand-sewn lace around the neck and seam joints of the arms and legs.

4 Join the head to the body by inserting the neck into the body and, with matching sewing thread, hemstitch it in place, adjusting the neck length and stuffing as necessary.

ARMS

5 Join the upper arm pieces to the lower arm pieces matching the balance marks, and then join the completed pieces together to form a pair leaving the top edge open as directed on the pattern piece. Trim the seam and carefully clip into the curved seam allowance around the hand.

6 Turn the arms through to the right side and stuff to within 2.5cm (1in) of the top. Turn in the top raw edge and make an inverted pleat at each side.

7 Pin the arms to the body at the shoulder line as indicated on the pattern making sure you arrange the arms so that the thumbs are facing front. Using matching thread, firmly oversew in place.

LEGS

8 Join the upper leg pieces to the lower leg pieces, matching the balance marks and then join the completed pieces together to form a pair, leaving the top and bottom edges open as directed on the pattern. Insert the sole into the base of the foot, matching the notches, then pin, tack and machine stitch around.

9 Carefully clip into the curved seams and turn the legs to the right side and stuff to within 2.5cm (1in) of the top. Turn in the raw edge, and then pin and tack across with the seams at the centre of the leg. Firmly oversew the legs to the body 13mm (½in) in front of the base seam to allow the doll to sit down. Finally, handsew the lace around the neck and the seam joins on the arms and legs.

FACE

10 Using the appropriate colours, embroider the eyes, nose and mouth using stranded embroidery cotton. Work the eyebrows in stem stitch using one strand of black. Then outline the eyes in stem stitch using two strands of black thread. Embroider the eyelashes in blanket stitch using one strand of black. And then fill in the pupils with satin stitch using two strands of black and the iris with two strands of blue.

11 Suggest the nostrils with two French knots using one strand of black thread. Fill in the lips using one strand of light red embroidery thread and satin stitch as shown. Then outline the mouth in stem stitch using one strand of deeper red.

12 Suggest the cheeks with a light dusting of blusher, practising first on an oddment of fabric to get just the right depth of pink.

HAIR

13 Cut the yarn in to equal lengths 80cm (32in) long. Using one of the lengths, tie the strands loosely together across the middle. Making this strand the centre parting, place the remaining strands over the head and sew them in place along the centre dotted line. Allowing about 10-12 strands for the fringe, spread the remaining yarn over the head and sew it in place along the hairline at the neck.

14 Bring all these strands up again and, using the red satin ribbon, tie them with a bow on top of the head. Trim the ends of the ponytail evenly. The fringe can be trimmed straight across or the long strands of yarn can be twisted together in groups to form curls. Do this by tightly twisting together one or two strands until they begin to twist on themselves. Fold in half, then place the raw ends under the curl, which will form when the yarn is "doubled" over. With a spot of clear adhesive, stick the yarn ends firmly to the head.

CLOTHING PATTERN PIECES

- Patterns for this project should be enlarged to twice the size. If you have access to a photocopier with an enlarging facility set it to 200%. Otherwise trace off the patterns on to a grid, following the procedure outlined on page 7.
- (See also the Checklist on page 112).

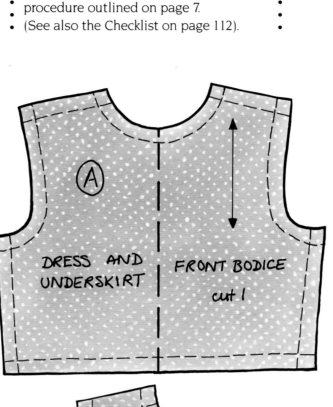

A

DRESS AND UNDERSKIRT — FRONT BODICE

cut 1

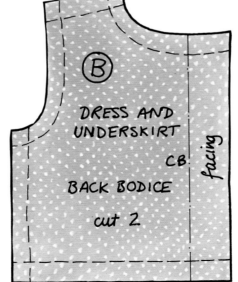

B

DRESS AND UNDERSKIRT

CB facing

BACK BODICE

cut 2

casing for elastic

E

PANTALOONS

cut 2

place on fold

trim line

hemline

D

COLLAR cut 4

Other pattern pieces:

From white lawn, cut the following rectangles on the
        straight grain.
Underskirt frills — one piece (H) 12cm x 76cm (4¾in x 30in)
                    two pieces (J) 18cm x 76cm (7in x 30in)
From white poplin, cut two cuff pieces (K), 5.5cm x 14.5cm
                                          (2¼in x 5¾in)
Cut one bias strip for the collar (L) 2.5cm x 18cm (1in x 7in)
From navy and white spotted fabric, cut the dress skirt (M)
            29cm x 104cm (11½in x 41in)

(G) SHOE SOLE
cut 2

(F) UPPER SHOE   cut 2

gather

(C) DRESS SLEEVE   cut 2

Cutting layout for white lawn fabric

Cutting layout for navy and white spotted fabric

CLASSIC CLOTH DOLL

Cutting layout for white poplin

The Clothes ~ Pantaloons

1 With the right sides inside, pin, tack and machine stitch the inner leg seams of each piece to form a pair. Place one leg inside the other and join the two legs together along the centre curved seam. Trim, clip into the curved seam and pull one leg through.

2 Make a narrow double turning at the ankle on each leg and machine stitch across. Then, pin, tack and machine stitch two decorative rows of lace trim as indicated on the pattern.

3 Make a double turning at the waist to form a casing for the elastic. Using an elastic threader or small safety pin, pass the elastic through the casing by unpicking a few stitches on the wrong side, and adjust it for the correct fit. Tie the elastic securely and stitch to close.

Underskirt

4 On each piece of the back bodice, fold in the centre facing, pin, tack and sew in place.

5 Join the back and front bodice pieces together at the shoulder seams. Press the seams open. Then machine stitch a length of 13mm (½in) wide white satin ribbon (left over from the belt) along the centre front. Apply two rows of narrow lace trim to each side, machine stitching them edge to edge for a neat finish. Cut out two or three flowers from the lace used to trim the doll seams, and hand sew them to the centre front, as shown in the diagram.

6 Turn in and tack the seam allowances around the edges of the neck and armholes. Covering the hems with the lace trim, pin, tack and machine stitch in place, overlapping the joins with a narrow turning at the underarm point.

7 Join the upper section of the underskirt with a centre back seam about 4cm (1½in) long. Neaten the opening above to match the bodice opening at the centre back.

8 With the right sides inside, join the side seams of the lower section of the underskirt. Press the seams open. Using a long stitch for gathering, machine a row of stitching along the top edges of both underskirt sections.

9 Pull up the underside thread and gather the top edge of the upper section to fit the bodice waist, evening the gathers. Then pin, tack and machine stitch in place. In the same way, gather the bottom section to fit the lower edge of the upper section and stitch in place.

10 Turn up the hem, pin and tack. Apply a row of lace trim, placing the straight edge just over the previous tacking stitches. Pin, tack and machine stitch to hold both the hem and trim in place.

11 Sew the press studs to the centre back bodice opening. Stitch the narrow ribbon to the waist at the centre back. In practice, this will cross and tie at the centre front.

DRESS

12 With right sides inside, begin by machine stitching the bodice backs to the bodice front at the shoulder seams. Trim to avoid bulky seams and press the seams open.

13 Construct the two collar sections by tacking and machine sewing the pieces together (in pairs) along the outer curved edges. Trim and clip into the seam, turn and press. Tack the lace trim in place along the outer edge and machine stitch.

14 Tack both collars in place along the neck edge. Fold back the facing to the right side and then tack and machine stitch the bias binding along the seamline. Turn under the opposite edge of the bias

binding and then pin and hem it to the neck seamline. Turn the facings to the wrong side and press carefully.

15 Gather the sleeve head between the notches. Gather the lower edge of the sleeve to fit the longer edge of the cuff. With right sides together, tack and machine stitch in place.

16 With right sides together, pin, tack and machine stitch the sleeves into the bodice armhole. Snip into the curved seams. Join the side seams and the underarm seams together in one continuous seam. Then turn the cuffs in half to the wrong side. Press and fold and hem in place.

17 Machine stitch the trim onto the skirt, placing the first row 8cm (3in) away from the lower raw edge and the second row 2.5cm (1in) above.

18 Stitch the centre back seam to within 9cm (3½in) of the waistline. Turn under the raw edges of the opening, machine stitch to neaten, and turn to the wrong side.

19 Following the instructions for making the underskirt, gather the waistline to fit the bodice. Pin, tack and machine stitch in place, omitting gathers from the facing.

20 Turn up the hem to the required length and, using matching thread, hem in place. Then sew press studs to the centre back opening to fasten and complete the dress.

STOCKINGS

21 Turn the child's socks inside out and pin the lower leg pattern in place, matching the centre front of the pattern to the front of the sock and the heel of the pattern to the heel of the sock.

22 With a pencil, draw around the pattern onto the sock and then machine stitch along the line using stretch machine stitch. Trim the excess fabric and turn right side out. Repeat for second stocking.

SHOES

23 With matching thread and using 4mm (⅛in) seam allowances throughout, machine stitch the centre back seam of each upper shoe. Insert the sole into the base of the shoe, tacking in place before machine stitching around. Leave the seams showing on the outside. Thread the narrow cord through the front straps to tie in a bow.

DEMONSTRATE YOUR DOLL-MAKING SKILLS WITH THIS SOPHISTICATED AND

DECORATIVE LADY. SHE MAKES A VERY ATTRACTIVE SPECIAL GIFT FOR AN OLDER

CHILD, TEENAGER OR ADULT - THAT IS, IF YOU CAN BEAR TO GIVE HER AWAY

ONCE YOU HAVE MADE HER!

BUTTON & BEAD DOLL

Button and bead joints make this doll a fascinating example of the doll-maker's art. Carefully postioned beads create knee and elbow joints and ensure the doll will sit gracefully on a shelf, desk or chair.

Buttons have been used to attach the legs to the body and thick thread attaches the arms – allowing them to move freely. The body is made in brightly patterned fabrics so that attaching a matching skirt and sleeves is quick to do and gives a striking overall effect.

Take special care with the face. Use the ingenious technique of tracing the features on the reverse of the face fabric and you will get perfect results.

Fabric for arms

Dress fabric

Fabric for legs

Bodice fabric

MATERIALS

DOLL (measures 43cm (17in) high)

- 20cm × 26cm (8in × 10in) of flesh-coloured cotton fabric (or calico) for the head, neck and shoulders
- 28cm × 26cm (11in × 10in) of small check cotton fabric for the top bodice and body
- 15cm × 20cm (6in × 8in) of plain toning coloured cotton fabric for the arms
- 30cm × 40cm (12in × 16in) of striped cotton fabric (in toning colours) for the legs
- Four macrame wooden beads, 1.5cm (⅝in) across with 6mm (¼in) wide holes, in natural wood colour, for the elbow and knee joints (if beads are not available, the joints can be made by gathering the fabric).
- Two buttons, 13mm (½in) across with two holes, for the hip joints
- 33g (1oz) of fine wool for the hair either knitting wool or tapisserie wool in a single colour or various shades of the same colour
- Polyester filling or kapok
- Long darning needle
- Pencil, or preferably an air-vanishing pencil for tracing on light fabric
- Dressmaker's chalk or yellow or silver marking pencil for tracing on dark fabrics
- Brown or black fine point permanent ink fabric pen or waterproof felt-pen for drawing the face details
- Acrylic or fabric paints in white, black, brown, red, yellow and blue eye colour for filling in the face details
- Fine paint brushes
- Acrylic varnish or white craft glue for sealing the paint
- Seam sealant, optional

DRESS

- 31cm (12in) of 90cm (36in) wide contrast patterned cotton fabric for the skirt and sleeves

DECORATION

- Embroidery threads and very fine ribbons for the shoe laces, bracelet and hair decorations
- Sufficient 2mm (⅛in) glass seed beads for the necklace and eight similar beads for the shoes

Calico for the body, and threads and fine ribbon for detailing

Buttons for the hip joints

Glass seed beading

Macrame beads for elbow and knee joints

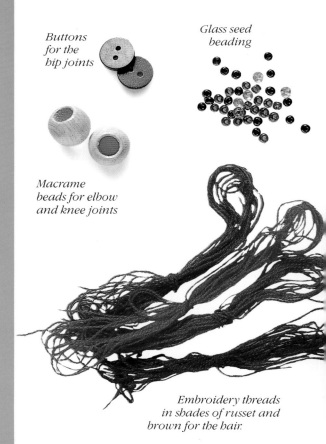

Embroidery threads in shades of russet and brown for the hair.

DOLL PATTERN PIECES

- Patterns for this project are life size and do not need to be enlarged. The body piece is shown overleaf. Before pinning on the pieces, see the Checklist also overleaf.

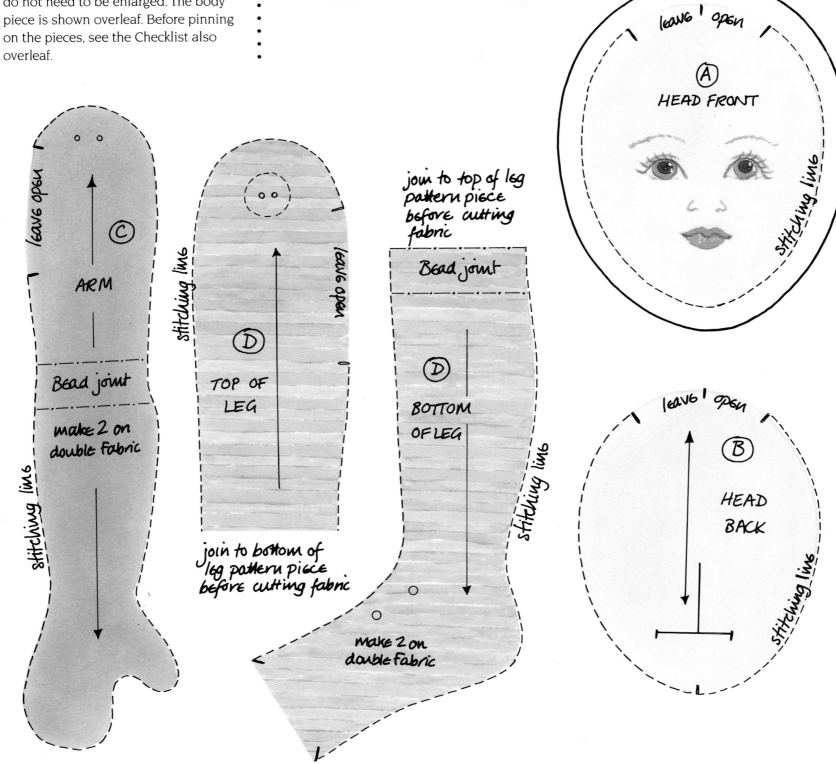

leave open

Ⓒ

ARM

Bead joint

make 2 on double fabric

stitching line

stitching line

Ⓓ

TOP OF LEG

leave open

join to bottom of leg pattern piece before cutting fabric

join to top of leg pattern piece before cutting fabric

Bead joint

Ⓓ

BOTTOM OF LEG

stitching line

make 2 on double fabric

leave open

Ⓐ

HEAD FRONT

stitching line

leave open

Ⓑ

HEAD BACK

stitching line

E

NECK
AND
SHOULDERS

seam line

stitching line

BODY
make 2 on
folded fabric

leave open

CHECKLIST

- Trace off the outline of the actual size pattern pieces. Transfer all marks and cut out, see pages 6-7.
- The body, arm and leg patterns show the stitching line only and seam allowances are added after stitching.
- Do not cut out the fabric pieces until instructed to do so.
- Press all fabrics: washing is optional as this doll is purely decorative.
- Set your sewing machine to the required stitch, check the length and tension and do a test run on your chosen fabric, see page 8.
- Use seam sealant sparingly on clipped curved seams to prevent fraying.
- Before painting the face details, test your paint on a spare piece of fabric.

THE DOLL ~

Note: the doll is made up in an unorthodox way whereby many of the doll pattern pieces show the stitching line only. Follow the instructions carefully observing that these pieces are stitched first and then cut out.

BODY

1 Cut a piece of flesh-coloured fabric, 10cm × 26cm (4in × 10in) wide and a piece of checked bodice fabric, 18cm × 26cm (7in x 10in) wide. With the right sides together, pin and machine stitch along one long edge. Press the seam allowances towards the patterned fabric.

Care and attention to detail are a feature of the front and back of the doll.

2 Fold the fabric widthways in half with the right sides together and seams matching. Place the body pattern centrally on the fabric, aligning the seamline on the paper with the seamline on the fabric, and allowing for 6mm (¼in) seams. Pin the pattern in place and draw around the outline.

3 Using matching sewing threads for each of the two fabrics, machine stitch around the body, leaving the opening as indicated on the pattern. Run a second line of machine stitching just outside the first one around the neck and shoulders to strengthen the seam.

4 Cut out the body adding a 6mm (¼in) seam allowance all round. Clip into the curved seams and use seam sealant if desired. Turn to the right side. Stuff very firmly, especially the neck area. Use a knitting needle to help push the filling in place. Oversew the opening to close.

ARMS

5 Fold the cotton fabric for the arms widthways in half. Trace around the arm pattern and repeat for the second arm allowing for 6mm (¼in) seams all round. Stitch as for the body. Make one or two horizontal stitches between the thumb and hand, for easy turning.

6 Cut out the arms trimming back the 6mm (¼in) seam allowance to 2mm (⅛in) around the hand and thumb. Clip into the curved seam allowances and apply seam sealant to the hand area. Turn to the right side.

7 Stuff the thumb first with tiny wisps of filling. Then stuff the hand fairly flat; begin to stuff more firmly at the wrist and continue with the lower arm until the first beadline as marked on the paper pattern. Roll the upper arm fabric lengthways and slip it through the wooden bead, pushing the bead down against the stuffing. If wooden beads are not available, run a gathering stitch along the elbow line, pull gathers and knot firmly. Repeat for the second arm ensuring that both elbows are evenly positioned. Stuff the upper arms a little less firmly. Using matching thread, close the opening.

LEGS

8 From the leg fabric, cut a piece measuring 30cm × 36cm (12in × 14in), making sure the stripes will run horizontally across the leg. Fold in half, with the right sides together, and draw around the pattern twice, as for the arms. Machine stitch around, leaving the two openings as indicated on the pattern.

9 Cut out the legs, adding 6mm (¼in) seam allowances. Clip into the curved seam between the leg and foot. Working on the wrong side, open out the foot area and fold flat, bringing the seams together in the centre. Mark a curved line for the toes as indicated in the illustration, pin and machine stitch. Trim the seam to 6mm (¼in) and turn to the right side.

10 Stuff the feet first, pushing the filling into all the corners with a knitting needle. Continue to stuff the lower leg up to the knee firmly. Slip beads on as indicated for the arm joints. Stuff the top of the leg firmly and close the opening with slipstitch.

HEAD AND FACE

11 From the remaining flesh-coloured fabric, cut a rectangle measuring 10cm x 20cm (4in × 8in). Place the face pattern on the wrong side of one half of the fabric leaving the other half for the back of the head. Trace around the oval shape only, with the vanishing pen. Mark the top and bottom positioning lines.

12 With the wrong side uppermost, place the face pattern under the fabric; align the positioning marks and pin to secure. Working against a window pane or on a lightbox, trace the features through to the wrong side of the fabric using a pencil. Remove the paper pattern.

13 Place the face fabric with the traced features down on to white paper where the lines pencilled on the reverse should be clearly distinguishable on the right side of the fabric.

14 With the brown permanent ink pen, carefully retrace the features on the right side of the fabric – the pupil can be suggested in black. Notice that the eyebrows are drawn with short strokes, rather than one continuous line.

PAINTING THE FACE

Note: always wait for the paint to dry thoroughly before applying further coats or adjacent colours.

15 With the right sides together, fold the face fabric in half and pin to secure. Machine stitch around 6mm (¼in) inside the marked outline leaving the opening at the top, as shown on the pattern. Cut out just inside the marked line. Place the back head pattern on the back head fabric. Transfer the positioning mark for attaching the head to the body.

16 Turn through to the right side. Stuff very firmly, smoothing out any creases along the curved edges. Neatly oversew the opening to close.

17 Begin by painting in the iris. Paint three-quarters of it, then add white to the eye colour and paint the "half past to quarter to" section of the iris in the lighter colour.

19 With white paint, lightly touch up the corners of the eyes outside the iris and put a highlight on each eye by painting a dot on the top right-hand quarter of each eye.

20 Finally, to seal and protect the paint, and also to add shine to the features, paint a layer of acrylic varnish or white craft glue on the eyes and mouth. This looks milky when wet but it will dry clear.

SOFT SCULPTURE

'A few "soft sculpture" stitches strategically placed give the face that degree of expression.

18 Then paint the mouth a pinky red and leave to dry. Add white to the lip colour to make it lighter and paint the upper part of the lower lip. Paint the pupil black. Using the brown pen go over the top line of the eyes to make them thicker.

21 With the darning needle threaded with doubled strong thread, start at the back of the head and sink the eye corners by taking a minute stitch at each eye corner. Make a second stitch at each point, pulling gently but not too tightly to get the desired effect. Make one stitch under the lower lip to get a chin effect, and knot securely at the back.

ASSEMBLING THE DOLL

22 Thread the darning needle with doubled strong thread and, following the diagram, begin by joining the legs to the body as follows. Insert the needle at point A, and bring it out at point B. Repeat at point C and D. Bring the needle out through one hole of the button and insert it again through the second hole. Return the needle through points D, C, B and A. Insert it again at E and bring it out at F. Attach the button as before and return the needle through points F and E. Repeat twice again until the stitching feels firm. Make a knot at a convenient hidden point such as A or B.

The hair can be decorated with tiny plaits, ribbons and beads.

23 Using doubled strong thread, join the arms to the body. Make the first stitch at the shoulder and a second stitch at the top of the arm. Repeat three or four times. Wind the thread around the stitches between the body and the arm, and work about three buttonhole stitches to secure the join. Stitch through the body and the arm once more and finally, secure the thread hiding the end inside the body. Repeat for the second arm.

24 To join the head to the body first cut through the fabric on the back of the head along the shape mark using small, sharp-pointed scissors. To make space for the neck remove a small amount of filling as necessary. Push the neck into the space with a turning movement and position the head as desired, straight or slightly inclined to one side. Make a narrow turning on the cut edges, pin in place, and oversew the head to the neck, stitching twice for a firm attachment.

HAIR

25 On a piece of paper, draw a line 6.5cm (2½in) long in the centre, parallel to the short edge. Cut 40cm (16in) lengths of wool and lay them across the line until there are sufficient to make a nice head of hair; the centre of the strands should be on the pencil line. Machine stitch twice through the wool and paper along the line, which will make the centre parting; secure the ends of the machine stitching firmly. Tear off the paper.

26 Pin the hair on the head, placing one end of the seam above the face at the centre hairline point, and the other end at the centre back neckline. Adjust, if necessary, and backstitch in place. Arrange the hair to cover the back of the neck; comb out with the fingers and trim to an even length. Embellish with ribbons or embroidery threads tied or plaited into her hair.

CLOTHING PATTERN PIECES

- Patterns for this project are life size and do not need to be enlarged. Before pinning on the pattern pieces, see the Checklist on page 122.

see the Checklist on page 122.

Other pattern pieces:

For the skirt, cut a rectangle 21.5cm × 61cm (8in × 24in) from patterned cotton fabric.

For the bodice, cut a rectangle 10cm × 20cm (4in × 8in) from the small checked cotton.

For the waistband, cut a length measuring 9cm × 23cm (3in × 9in) from fabric to match the skirt.

THE CLOTHES ~ SKIRT

1 From the skirt fabric cut a rectangle measuring 21cm × 60cm (8½in × 24in). Join the short edges right sides together, pin and machine stitch. Press the seams open. Make a double turning at the hem, 1cm (⅜in) deep and machine stitch in place.

2 Using a long machine stitch, run a line of gathering stitches along the waist edge of the skirt. Pull up the gathers and fit the skirt on the doll. Secure the threads, even out the gathers, and pin the skirt in place. Backstitch to the doll, stitching through the gathered line.

Ⓐ

SLEEVE

cut 2

place on fold

3 For the waistband, cut a length of skirt fabric measuring 23cm x 9cm (9in × 3½in). Machine stitch a 6mm (¼in) hem on both short sides. With the wrong sides together, fold lengthways in half and press, open up, and fold each half towards the centre and press again. Pin together and topstitch around all four edges. Place on the waist to cover the raw edges of skirt, crossing over the ends at the back. Pin and hem stitch to the skirt.

BODICE TOP

4 From the remaining bodice fabric, cut a rectangle measuring 20cm × 10cm (8in × 4in). With the fabric right side down, fold the long edges inwards so that it is about 4.5cm (1¾in) wide. Press. Using double thread, run a central gathering line across the width. Pull up the gathers and secure the thread. Pin the bodice top in place with the gathers to the centre front. Overlap the edges of the back and neatly hem stitch to close.

SLEEVES

5 Cut out two sleeves from the remaining skirt fabric. With the right sides facing, pin and machine stitch the two short edges together. Press the seam open and turn to the right side. Run a machine gathering line along both long edges, 6mm (¼in) from the edge. Pull up the gathers on the sleeve head, turn under the raw edge and fit the sleeve on the doll with the underarm seam below the arm. Pin in place and oversew the sleeve to the doll at the shoulder. Pull up the gathers at the bottom of the sleeve, turn under the raw edge and hand stitch the sleeve to the arms, just above the bead joint. Repeat all the above for the second sleeve.

SHOES

6 Stitch four beads on each of the feet where indicated, and thread a length of a thin ribbon or thick embroidery thread around them crossing in front as for laceup shoes. Tie in a bow to finish.

NECKLACE AND BRACELET

7 Thread the remaining small beads onto a short length of embroidery thread, to make a necklace about 13cm (5in) long, and tie around the doll's neck, finishing with a bow at the back. Make the bracelet by tying a length of very narrow ribbon or thick embroidery thread around the doll's wrist.

Sleeves and skirt are gathered and stitched straight onto the body.

$\mathcal{S}$TITCH GLOSSARY

The following instructions explain in detail how to work the various stitches which are involved in making the doll projects.

Backstitch can be used for hand sewing a seam or a decorative embroidery stitch.

Bring the thread through on the stitch line, then make a small backward stitch to the right. Pass the needle forward under the fabric and bring it out one stitch length ahead, ready to make the next stitch. Make all the stitches the same length.

Blanket stitch gives a decorative finish to the edge of a garment.

Working from left to right, bring the needle out on the bottom line. Insert it above (the required depth of the stitch away) just to the right and bring it out immediately below, with the needle over the working thread. Continue in the same way making the stitches and the spaces between the same size, and keeping the purled edge of the stitch on the outer edge of the fabric.

Slit buttonhole: the raw edges are finished with buttonhole stitch.

First run small stitches around the slit to the depth of both rows of buttonholing. Make two straight stitches at one end and, working from right to left, bring the thread out through the slit. Insert the needle from behind and bring it out just below the outline stitches with the thread under the needle. Take the thread back to the top edge and continue in this way to the end of the slit. Work one or two straight stitches across the end, turn the buttonhole around and complete the second side.

Chain stitch is a decorative embroidery stitch used for outlining and solid infilling.

Bring out the thread on the stitch line and hold it down to the left. Insert the needle at the starting point and bring it out a short distance below with the

thread under the needle. Pull the needle through to form the first chain and repeat the stitch along the line.

Feather stitch is a decorative embroidery stitch used for outlines and borders.

Bring the needle out on the stitch line and, with the thread held to the left, insert it a little way down to the right. Bring it out again directly below the starting point. Make a similar stitch to the left, on the same level, and continue working these two stages alternately.

French knots can be used singly to suggest nostrils and other face details as well as decorative stitch borders.

Bring out the thread where the knot is to be worked. Hold it down with the left thumb and, with the needle, encircle the thread twice. Twist the needle back to the

starting point and insert it close to where the thread emerged. Pull the needle through to the back and repeat as needed.

Gathering stitches can be made either by machine or hand.

Sewing machine: lengthen the straight sewing stitch as required. Stitch and then pull up the lower thread to form the gathers. Knot firmly to secure.
Hand: with a long length of sewing thread in the needle make small to medium size running stitches along the entire length of the line to be gathered. Pull up as needed. It is important to begin with sufficient thread as knots will not allow the fabric to gather.

Hem stitch (hemming stitch) can be used to secure all types of hem by hand.

With the hem tacked in place, bring out the thread on the wrong side. Holding the needle at a diagonal take a tiny stitch in the fabric first and then insert it upwards to take a small stitch in the hem fold. Pull through and repeat spacing the stitches evenly about 5mm ($^3/_{16}$in) apart.

Herringbone stitch can be used in embroidery or as a catch stitch to hold facings in place.

Working from left to right, make a small horizontal stitch in the upper layer of fabric, then a small horizontal stitch in the lower layer diagonally across the first stitch. Continue in this way keeping the thread loose.

Long and short stitch is used as a filling stitch in embroidery

Work the first row in alternate long and short straight stitches following the outline of the area to be filled. Work the next and subsequent rows in straight stitches of equal length.

Oversew (whipstitch) is used to close an opening and to join two separate sections such as attaching a limb to the body of a doll.

Working from right to left, take the needle diagonally over the edges of the fabric, picking up a few fabric threads only, and bring it through to the front again. Repeat as needed making small evenly spaced diagonal stitches.

Satin stitch is an infilling stitch used in embroidery.

Working from the bottom left to the top right, embroider straight stitches diagonally across the area to be filled. The stitches should fit close together, all at the same angle and should form straight outside edges.

Slip stitch is used to join a folded edge to another fold or single layer of fabric. It is almost invisible since the larger part of each stitch is concealed within the fabric.

Working from right to left, bring the needle through on the fold, take it over into the fabric below (or into the opposite fold) picking up a single thread. Return the needle into the first folded edge and bring it out a short distance away. Repeat as needed.

Stem stitch is a line stitch used in embroidery.

Bring the needle out on the stitch line. Working from left to right, hold the thread down with the left thumb and make a small stitch to the right bringing the needle out a short distance towards the left. Repeat along the stitch line making the stitch at a slight angle to the stitch line to produce a broad twisted effect.

Stretch machine stitch is used for seaming stretch fabrics.

While some sewing machines have a special stitch, ordinary zigzag stitch will do the job just as well. Use the narrowest stitch, and do a test run to make sure it will "give" with the fabric.

Tacking stitch is used to temporarily hold together two or more fabric layers during the construction of a project.

Working from right to left, take several evenly spaced stitches onto the needle before pulling through. Use smaller even tacking stitches in areas that require close control and use longer uneven tacking stitches for general purposes such as during permanent stitching.

Zigzag stitch is a wide decorative border stitch used in embroidery.

Bring the needle out on the upper stitch line. Working from right to left, insert the needle on the lower stitch line a short distance to the right. Making a horizontal stitch to the left, bring the needle out on the lower line a short distance beyond the level of the starting point. Reinsert the needle into the starting point and make a similar stitch on the top stitch line. Continue to the end of the row repeating the sequence.

INDEX

$\mathcal{I}$NDEX

USEFUL ADDRESSES

International mail order addresses for general doll-making supplies.
Catalogue available on request

United Kingdom
Children's Treasures
17 George Street
Hastings
East Sussex
TN34 3EG
Telephone/facsimile: (0424) 444117

Pick N' Choose
The Craft People
56 Station Road
Northwich
Cheshire
CW9 5RB
Telephone: (0606) 41523

United States
A Dollmaker's Marketplace
P.O. Box 110280
Campbell
CA 95011
Telephone: 1/800/328-3655

Australia
Sarah Sey Dolls and Crafts
39 Annangrove Road
Kenthurst
New South Wales 2156
Telephone/facsimile: (02) 654 2181